The New Local Government Series
No. 5

THE *REFORMED* LOCAL GOVERNMENT SYSTEM

The New Local Government Series

Series Editor: Professor Peter G. Richards

THE *REFORMED* LOCAL GOVERNMENT SYSTEM

BY

PETER G. RICHARDS

Professor of British Government
University of Southampton

London
GEORGE ALLEN & UNWIN
Boston   Sydney

First published in 1973
Second edition 1975
Second impression 1976
Third edition 1978
Fourth edition 1980

GEORGE ALLEN & UNWIN LTD
40 Museum Street, London WC1A 1LU

© George Allen & Unwin (Publishers) Ltd 1973,
1975, 1978, 1980

ISBN 0 04 352 068 5 paperback

British Library Cataloguing in Publication Data

Richards, Peter Godfrey
    The reformed local government system. 4th-ed. –
(The new local government series; no. 5).
    1. Local government – England
    I. Title
    352.042   JS3091   80–40348

ISBN 0–04–352090–1

Printed in Great Britain by
Biddles Ltd. Guildford. Surrey

PREFACE

The Local Government Act, 1972, takes effect on 1 April 1974. It provides for the most radical change in our local government system since 1888. In particular, the basic distinction then created between counties and county boroughs has disappeared. The new divide is between metropolitan and non-metropolitan areas. In these circumstances a fresh introductory volume was needed for George Allen & Unwin's series of books on local government, replacing my volume *The New Local Government System*. More than that, the series required a new title, for the old name *The Town and County Hall* Series reflected the importance of the county/county borough division that has gone. So this volume introduces a fresh series title, *The New Local Government Series*.

The purpose of this book is to provide students and all those interested in public affairs with an explanation of why fundamental change was needed, together with a description of the new institutions and of the political, social, economic and administrative framework in which they operate. Over the years the study of local government has developed a much broader content. The original introductory volume to this series, *The English Local Government System* by the late J. H. Warren was first published in 1946 and was concerned almost wholly with law and administration. Now many other aspects of the subject must be included. Party politics has a much greater effect on local government than in the immediate post-war period, partly because of political activity at local elections and partly because of the close relationship between central and local government. There is a stronger sociological element in the study of local government as we have become more conscious of the effect of behaviour patterns on the working of formal institutions. There is also growing concern with management. The study of management techniques is basically an examination of administrative method, but the tendency to think in terms of 'management' rather than 'administration' is more than a change of fashion in the use of words, because management does imply a continuous quest for efficiency. So this book, granted the limitations imposed by its length, attempts to bring together political, sociological and managerial approaches to local government.

It will be clear to all readers that this work looks to the future.

PREFACE

What is described here is not local government as it exists on the day of publication but as it will be under the new Act.

I am grateful, indeed continuously grateful, to Mrs Dunn and Mrs Powell, who do my typing with great care, and to Miss Diana Marshallsay, B.A., Dip.Lib., who gave advice and assistance with the index. My wife carried out her customary task of putting a final polish on the material before it went to the printer.

PETER G. RICHARDS

University of Southampton

PREFACE TO THE SECOND EDITION

The favourable reception given to this book has now created the need for a new edition. Substantial changes have been made. These reflect events over the past two years and, in particular, some problems of bringing the reformed system of local government into operation on 1 April 1974.

PETER G. RICHARDS

University of Southampton
November 1974

PREFACE TO THE THIRD EDITION

The need for a further edition provides an opportunity to keep a book fully up to date. Perhaps the major event in local government in the last two years has been the Layfield Report. Accordingly Chapters V and VIII have been substantially revised to take account of the Layfield recommendations.

University of Southampton   PETER G. RICHARDS
July 1977

PREFACE TO THE FOURTH EDITION

Local government continues to experience change, not mainly in terms of new structures or extra duties, but because of alterations in the policy of central government. Revisions in the text for the fourth edition stem very largely from ministerial initiative—particularly arising from the election of a Conservative Government.

University of Southampton   PETER G. RICHARDS
December 1979

CONTENTS

CONTENTS

Chapter I

INTRODUCTION THROUGH HISTORY

The present system of local government in England and Wales cannot be fully appreciated without reference to the past. Yet the history of local government is a vast subject on its own—witness the magnificent works of Sidney and Beatrice Webb. In an introductory book the historical element must be a mere sketch. This chapter is a sketch of the development of local government, but one that concentrates on the interrelationship of local administrative areas, local services and local resources. It also tries to link the growth of local services with the dominant trends in political thought at least since 1834. How people react to social problems depends on what they feel to be morally right: the moral drive behind much of local government is one aspect too often overlooked.

TRADITIONAL UNITS AND THEIR DECLINE

The three traditional units of local government in England and Wales have been the county, the parish and the borough. Each has had its own functions which were exercised with a large degree of independence, although the county justices had supervisory powers over parish officers. However, the sense of separateness was so strong that the idea of a *local government system* with major and minor local authorities with interlocking responsibilities did not emerge clearly until the latter part of the nineteenth century. By modern standards, the local units of government also suffered little central control. Central interference varied with the political situation of the time—the later Stuart Kings, in particular, tried to ensure that local positions of influence were held by their supporters—but local institutions were left to deal with local problems in the way they thought best. Since national grants were unknown until the eighteen-forties, the scale of county, parish and borough activity was minimal. Indeed, much effort was expended in the eighteenth century on the promotion of new local bodies to carry out tasks which the traditional authorities were unable or unwilling to undertake.

The county has its origins in feudal times when it was the territory granted by the King to an earl in return for acceptance of feudal obligations. After the feudal period justices of the peace chosen through the King's representative, the Lord Lieutenant, became responsible for county government. Initially the justices were essentially concerned with the maintenance of law and order. Thus their functions were primarily judicial. However, they had some administrative responsibilities, mainly for prisons and bridges, and they had to settle disputes arising out of the actions of parish officers. Visiting justices made irregular visits to parishes to inspect their poor law accounts.

Boroughs were based on charters granted at different times by the monarchy. These charters were valuable because they gave a small town the right to have its own justices and, therefore, to have its own court: this saved much difficulty and expense since disputes could be settled locally and without the need for a possibly unpleasant journey to the quarter sessions. Charters also gave the right to hold markets and so assisted trade and prosperity. They also provided for separate parliamentary representation, but this was commonly regarded as a mixed blessing because of the cost and danger of travel to Westminster. Often borough charters were granted by the King in the expectation of being able to control the nominations to the House of Commons made by the borough. The borough corporations themselves were usually renewed through a process of self-co-option.

The parish was originally the smallest unit of church organisation. It gradually acquired non-ecclesiastical functions, starting with highways in the sixteenth century and the care of the poor in 1601. Frequently the word 'vestry' was used instead of parish because meetings to discuss parish business were held in the church vestry. The names 'open vestry' and 'closed vestry' described how far parish business was open to all parishioners; in a closed vestry decisions would be taken by the local elite—the people who were the largest ratepayers in the parish. Whether any particular vestry was open or closed generally depended on local convention rather than law.

For the common people the parish became the most important local unit of government as it had the greatest effect on their lives. The ancient liability that highways should be repaired 'by the inhabitants at large' was enforced through the parish. By the Statute of Highways, 1555, each parish had to appoint two surveyors responsible for the repair of roads in the parish, and the inhabitants were required to devote four days labour to this work of maintenance. The more wealthy members of the community chose to pay a highway rate instead of doing the work themselves and the money collected was used to pay the poor for working on the roads. The administrative duties of the parish became truly burdensome after 1601 when it was made responsible for the relief of the poor. The

Elizabethan poor law required each parish to appoint an overseer who would impose a rate on the local inhabitants to raise money for the purchase of materials on which the poor could be put to work. The theory was that the goods made would be sold and the revenue could then be distributed to relieve poverty. Thus the poor would be helped, but they would also have to work to help themselves. The theory was commendable, but in practice, the idea could not work. The administration required was too complex for an unpaid parish officer to carry out: even where working materials were provided, paupers were often so old, ill or unskilled, or living in such bad conditions that useful work could not be done. The scheme collapsed and was replaced by the gratuitous distribution of relief financed by a parish rate. Especially in times of bad trade the cost of the poor law was heavy and often caused dispute within a parish.

Each parish carried out its duties through four types of unpaid officer—the overseer of the poor, the surveyor, the constable and the churchwarden. The duties of the first two have already been described. The constable was responsible for keeping the peace and took offenders before the magistrates. The churchwarden was responsible for the maintenance of the fabric of the parish church and, if necessary, collected a rate from the parish to pay for this to be done. Often the necessary funds were subscribed by the wealthy and church rates were rarely required. Necessarily they provoked opposition and indignation from nonconformists who did not attend the parish church. In 1837 the Braintree vestry refused to agree to a church rate and when the churchwarden tried to collect the money without authority his action was successfully challenged in the courts. In 1868 the Gladstone Liberal government abolished church rates and cut another link between ecclesiastical and civil administration.

The parish officers were appointed at the vestry meeting. Since the work was substantial in amount and sometimes unpleasant, it was not always easy to find persons willing to serve. However, the system worked because of a general feeling that good citizens should accept a share of social responsibility. Often the jobs were passed round at the end of a year's duty. Some parishes had an understanding that a parish officer could nominate his successor. The overseer had the heaviest task and in some places a payment was made to him for his trouble; this might be done quite unofficially by means of private donations from the well-to-do inhabitants. Yet the whole system depended on part-time service and goodwill. It was quite unable to accept any wider responsibilities, so when demands came forward for extra and improved local administration the parish was by-passed. More efficient and more complex social provision required better qualified, paid and full-time staff which, in turn, required a larger unit of organisation than the parish. Equally, the county and the borough were ill-placed to obtain extra duties, especially those involving the expenditure of public money. They were not representative bodies and not responsible to the public. So there were obvious grounds for refusing them any further taxing powers. In addition, some borough corporations and, indeed, some magistrates in urban areas were widely accused of corruption—of using official positions to secure personal gain. In the pre-railway age the larger counties were also regarded as too large a unit to be convenient for local administration.

Since the parish, the county and the borough were unsuitable to deal with the social problems arising from the growth of trade, the industrial revolution and the growth of population, new local government institutions were created. The three most important were the turnpike trusts, the Improvement Commissioners and the poor law unions.

The turnpikes were urgently needed to improve the state of the roads. In the eighteenth century there was a dramatic increase in the amount of road transport largely because of more trade but also because people started to travel more for pleasure or for health reasons. To place responsibility for maintaining roads on the parish was both inefficient and unfair. The largest parishes in terms of area were normally those in sparsely populated countryside, while the smaller parishes were in the more thickly populated districts. There was no correlation between the resources of a parish in terms of money or labour and the extent of its highway responsibilities: a parish with a tiny population could have a long stretch of a road running through it which linked major towns. Turnpike trusts were established by Acts of Parliament to charge tolls on travellers for using a road and the proceeds of the tolls could meet the cost of repairing the roads. Today many old toll houses can still be seen situated by the side of main roads.

The growth of towns aggravated many problems of urban living. As in the countryside there was a greater need to maintain roads, but there was also a need for drainage and for the effective maintenance of law and order, particularly the prevention of robbery. Many of the new industrial towns had no municipal corporation: elsewhere the corporations were in the hands of a limited clique and were not respected by the greater part of the citizens. So throughout the country bodies of Improvement Commissions were established by locally sponsored Acts of Parliament. The Commissioners were nominated in the local Act and renewed by co-option, but by the early days of the nineteenth century the principle of ratepayer election was introduced. Their powers varied and were defined in each local

Act. In towns adjacent to rivers or the sea they often provided docking facilities and were known as Harbour and Improvement Commissioners. In general, they were responsible for lighting, paving and draining streets and for providing a watch—an embryonic police force.

Undoubtedly, the most expensive and most contentious branch of local administration was poor relief. During the eighteenth century the parish was already losing control of this function. Various Acts strengthened the power of the justices to supervise the distribution of relief. In 1795 the magistrates of Speenhamland drew up a scale of payments which related the amount of relief payable to the size of a pauper's family and to the price of bread; this Speenhamland scale was widely adopted by justices and overseers. Parliament also permitted parishes to work together in dealing with the poor. An Act of 1723 allowed parishes to join together and form unions which could build workhouses where the poor could live and work. This power was not widely used but another Act of 1782 authorised parishes to join together in unions so they could appoint paid officers to carry out the distribution of relief. These poor law unions were controlled by Guardians, originally appointed by the justices, but subsequently elected by ratepayers.

Two features dominated the law of local administration—it was both local and permissive. Only some main traffic routes were cared for by turnpikes; others were covered partially or not at all. Only some parishes agreed to join poor law unions. The powers of Improvement Commissioners varied as did their relationship, if any, with the local municipal corporation. Until late in the nineteenth century nothing existed that could be described as a coherent system of local services—instead there was a chaos of institutions, areas and rates.

NINETEENTH-CENTURY REFORM

The political upheaval which produced the 1832 Reform Bill had an immediate impact on local administration. The first major change concerned the poor law. In 1832 a Poor Law Commission was appointed to report on the working of the existing arrangements and the Commission sent out investigators to examine conditions in about 300 parishes. These investigators may be considered as the forerunners of the present-day inspectorate. The Commission's Report portrayed a situation of confusion, incompetence and waste. The Poor Law Amendment Act, 1834, based on the Commission's recommendations, provided a new and uniform basis for poor relief. A central body in London, the Poor Law Commission, was to supervise the whole system—the start of central control over the detailed administration of local services. The central body united parishes into convenient areas for poor law purposes and in so doing ignored other traditional divisions. Thus many unions overlapped county boundaries. The poor law unions were also *ad hoc* bodies, i.e. they were formed to carry out a particular service. This was not a new idea in 1834 for turnpikes had then existed for many years, but the poor law unions were the first example of a pattern of *ad hoc* authorities covering the whole country; now there are many examples of this kind, water and health authorities and the area organisations of public corporations. The Poor Law Commission laid down strict rules covering the distribution of relief. The unions were to build workhouses and the distribution of relief other than to the inmates of the workhouse was banned: the regime in the workhouse was to be spartan to deter applications for admission. Local Boards of Guardians were elected by the ratepayers to run the workhouses, subject to national control.

The other major reform of the eighteen-thirties applied to the municipal corporations. Once more a Commission of enquiry was appointed and Assistant Commissioners were sent out to examine how the corporations were conducted. Again the Report was damning. Some corporations were so decayed as to be virtually non-existent; many did nothing of value for the local inhabitants; some were corrupt. The Municipal Corporations Act, 1835, gave the boroughs a new constitution and insisted on proper financial management. Borough councillors were to be elected by the ratepayers and the House of Lords required that a quarter of the council should consist of aldermen elected by the councillors. All borough revenues were to be paid into a single fund to be used for the benefit of the inhabitants. The administration of justice was divorced from the administration of services and the borough justices were separated from the borough council. But in contrast to the Poor Law Amendment Act, the amount of central control was negligible. The major task of the borough was the maintenance of law and order and the 1835 Act decreed that a quarterly report from the local Watch Committee be submitted to the Home Secretary. A borough could also make bye-laws for the good rule and government of its area which were subject to approval of the Privy Council. The Treasury was empowered to stop the sale and long leases of corporation-owned land. Yet the total effect of these controls was small. The 1835 Act did nothing to change the area of boroughs. It was applied to 178 towns. Other places which claimed borough status were ignored and the corporations deprived of recognition faded away. The City of London also managed to avoid coming under these provisions:

many attempts in the following fifty years to reform London government were frustrated by the powerful financial interests of the City.

These two Acts demonstrate a remarkable difference of approach.
The poor law reform was based on central control, uniformity,
rationalisation of areas and the *ad hoc* principle. The Municipal
Corporations Act emphasised the authority of local representatives
subject to a minimum of central direction, maintained existing areas
and created an organisation capable of dealing with a wide range of
services. All these contrasts recur in the subsequent history of local
government. Indeed, they form the basis of much of the recent
discussion about the shape of future local government reform.

In the eighteen-forties public attention was concentrated on the
question of health. This concern was largely stimulated by Edwin
Chadwick, Secretary of the Poor Law Commissioners, who was
convinced that disease was the main cause of poverty, and that the
best way to help the poor was to remove the causes of sickness.
Reports of official enquiries, heavily influenced by Chadwick, slowly
created public willingness for government action. The two major
reports on the Sanitary Condition of the Labouring Population
(1842) and the State of Large Towns (1845) revealed almost unbeliev-
able conditions of filth, squalor and a lack of drainage and pure
water supplies. The Public Health Act, 1848, authorised the establishment of local Boards of Health to provide water supply and drainage,
either where the inhabitants requested it or where the death rate
exceeded 23 per 1,000. Municipal Corporations became the Boards
of Health for their own areas. The work of the local Boards was to
be supervised by a Central Board of Health. Earlier, in 1846, the
Poor Law Guardians had been given limited powers to deal with
insanitary nuisances in rural areas.

The public health legislation to a large extent followed the model
of the poor law reform. However, there were differences, which
grew larger as time passed. The element of central control was present
and more *ad hoc* bodies were created. However, more scope was
allowed for local initiative and the Central Board of Health never
achieved the dominance of the Poor Law Commission. The Central
Board was reorganised in 1854 and dissolved in 1858, its functions
being divided between the Privy Council and the Home Office. (The
original Poor Law Commission had been displaced in 1847 by a
Minister, the President of the Poor Law Board, who was directly
answerable to Parliament: but the central direction of poor relief
remained firm.) The opposition to central direction on health questions was due to the disappearance of epidemics and the dislike of
spending large sums of money that had to be raised by local taxation.
Yet even when the *laissez-faire* reaction swept away the Central

Board of Health in 1858 there remained 670 local Boards of Health which continued to promote more civilised conditions in urban areas.

After a decade of inaction at national level, the Royal Sanitary Commission was appointed in 1868. Its Report in 1871 set out the requirements 'of what is necessary for a civilised social life' which included a pure water supply, sewage, burial arrangements and the inspection of food. A new government department, the Local Government Board, was created in 1871 to deal with these matters. In 1872 the whole country was divided up into urban and rural sanitary districts, the urban authorities being given wider powers. The urban authorities were boroughs, Improvement Commissioners and local Boards of Health: Poor Law Guardians became sanitary authorities for the parts of their union not included in the above. Thus while the Guardians combined both town and country for poor law purposes, they dealt with public health matters solely in the countryside. This separation of urban and rural areas was a reversal of one of the principles of the 1834 poor law reform and created the basis of the later distinction between urban and rural districts.

At this period the question of highway maintenance became acute as the turnpike trust system was breaking down. The new steam railways provided an alternative means of transport and adversely affected the revenues of the turnpikes, so reducing their ability to keep roads in good repair. There was also increased public opposition to the payment of tolls. In South Wales rioters destroyed turnpike gates. Consequently Parliament refused to renew the powers of the turnpike trusts when they lapsed and the disturnpiked roads reverted to the care of the parish. Even in the eighteenth century it had been widely accepted that the parish was not competent to maintain the roads and the obvious need was for the creation of a highway authority based on a larger unit than the parish. The county was unacceptable since the county justices were not elected. The alternative was to form unions of parishes on the model of the poor law. In 1862 the county justices were given powers to create such unions, but often these were based on the areas of the justices' petty sessional districts, not on the areas of the poor law unions. This added substantially to the confusion of local administration in rural areas. Highway districts were highly unpopular. They imposed a financial obligation upon the parish rate which had no connection with the extent of the traditional liability of the parish to maintain its own roads. Parishes suffered if small in area with substantial population; parishes gained if large in area with a small population. In some cases the gains and losses were heavy. Many large villages managed to opt out of a highway district by adopting the Public

Health Act, 1848, and forming their own local Board of Health which entitled them to separate highway powers. In 1863 this trick was stopped by an Act which stipulated that only parishes with a population of at least 3,000 could adopt the Public Health Act. Meanwhile some very small pre-1974 urban districts owed their existence to the scramble to avoid inclusion in a highway union. The resistance to highway unions was so acute that in some areas they were never formed. In other places they were allowed to decay and responsibility for the roads again fell back on the parish. Elsewhere the areas were rationalised and made to conform with the poor law unions, yet this was often difficult because the poor law unions frequently overlapped county boundaries.

Today many local authority areas are anomalous: in the nineteenth century they were fantastic. Over a thousand parishes included one or more parcels of land completely detached from the main body of the parish; in the west of England the separated parts were occasionally situated in a different county. This jigsaw necessarily complicated local administration. The parish of Threapwood in the Wrexham poor law union was partly in Cheshire and partly in Denbighshire and so was part in England and part in Wales. A woman in the village, a pauper, went mad and had to be sent to an asylum. In England the charge for maintaining a pauper lunatic was 14s a week, in Wales it was only 8s a week. The question arose whether the woman was domiciled in the English or the Welsh sector of the village. The Clerk of the Wrexham Union discovered that the house where the woman was born was astride the county boundary. However, he was able to establish that the woman was born in the Welsh piece of the house and so saved his authority 6s a week. This cameo is drawn from evidence presented to the Select Committee on Parish, Union and County Boundaries which reported in 1873. Gradually parish boundaries were rationalised, but the process was slow.

Parish boundaries achieved greater impórtance because of both roads and education. In 1870 Gladstone's first Liberal Government imposed on the parish the responsibility of providing a school if an adequate one had not been provided by voluntary agencies—i.e. the churches. School attendance became compulsory in 1876 and free in 1891. The eccentric boundaries had effects which appeared inequitable. The main part of a parish could have a satisfactory church school but no provision for children in a detached piece some distance off; the whole parish was required to contribute to the provision of a school for the detached part. Even in 1870 the parish was obviously too small a unit to be a satisfactory education authority. However, since many parishes already had schools it was impossible to create school unions in which the cost could be pooled: such an arrangement would have aroused even more antagonism than the highway unions.

Over the years various pressures developed which made a democratic reform of county government long overdue. Agricultural labourers gained the parliamentary franchise through the third Reform Bill, 1884. The anomaly that boroughs, but not counties, enjoyed representative government had existed for half a century. The administrative duties of the county justice had grown steadily and so had the size of the county rate demand. In particular, the village constable was replaced by the county police force in 1856. It became clear that further services, notably highways, ought to be made a county responsibility in order to achieve better and more uniform standards of repair and to spread the cost over a wider area. Finally, administration in the London area was seriously in need of reform. London had grown far beyond the area of the City, which had successfully avoided all attempts to modernise its constitution. Many important services were provided by the Metropolitan Board of Works established in 1855 which was based on a system of indirect election through a pattern of district boards. The Metropolitan Board had been responsible for substantial redevelopment in the West End but had become corrupt. Beyond question, London needed unified and democratic local government. These pressures, combined with the influence of Joseph Chamberlain and the Liberal Unionists within Lord Salisbury's Conservative Government, succeeded in making a major reform. The Local Government Act, 1888, remained the foundation of our present system of local government—outside London—until the coming into force of the Local Government Act, 1972.

The 1888 Act had three major aspects. It created a new system of county councils elected on a ratepayer franchise; it defined the relationship between the county councils and the boroughs; it reorganised the financial relations between central and local government. When originally introduced the Bill had a further section covering the reform of smaller authorities within the county, but this had to be dropped for lack of parliamentary time. After a delay of six years this part of the reform was enacted in 1894.

The new county councils did not correspond entirely with the historic counties. Some were divided for administrative convenience because of the size of the county, e.g. Yorkshire, or its shape, e.g. Sussex. To a great extent these divisions often represented existing practice in that the county magistrates had met in separate centres and had levied separate rates. The bisection of Suffolk was based on acceptance of current arrangements. The problem of the metropolis was solved by carving a new county, the London County Council, out of Middlesex, Surrey and Kent, the LCC boundaries being based on those of the superseded Metropolitan Board of Works. Two years after the Act was passed the Isle of Wight was also made a separate county. Thus the trisection of Yorkshire and Lincolnshire, the division of Cambridgeshire, Northamptonshire, Hampshire, Suffolk and Sussex, together with the new county of London created a total of 62 county councils out of the 52 geographical counties.

Initially the powers given to the counties were limited. Their major task was to care for those roads designated as county roads. A joint committee was formed with the county justices to supervise the county police force. They also inherited from the county justices an assortment of administrative duties, many relating to the issue of licences for various purposes. In subsequent years the counties acquired a wide range of functions. Indeed, the history of local government in the twentieth century can be largely summarised by listing the extensions to county responsibilities.

Much parliamentary time was consumed by the representatives of boroughs fighting for their independence from the new county councils. As originally drafted the Bill excluded only the very largest towns with a population of 150,000 from the aegis of the counties. This implied that all other boroughs would be subordinate to the county councils and would have to pay the county rate. Previously boroughs with their own quarter sessions had been exempt from the county rate because the administrative duties of the county justices had been carried out by their own borough bench. Under pressure from borough MPs the size of boroughs with county powers—i.e. county boroughs—was reduced to 50,000 population, and four smaller boroughs, Burton-on-Trent, Canterbury, Chester and Worcester, were also admitted to the select band.

The financial sections of the 1888 Act were an attempt to secure some order and principle for methods of giving monetary aid to local authorities. At various dates since the Chadwick era Exchequer grants had been given in respect of education, police, highways, criminal prosecutions and some aspects of the poor law. The grants were designed to encourage better standards of provision in these fields and had grown steadily in amount. To place a limit on the cost of these grants to the national taxpayer, it was agreed that most of the specific grants mentioned above be replaced by a single combined grant, to be paid from a separate Local Taxation Account. This Account was to be supplied with 40 per cent of the product of certain national taxes—the so-called assigned revenues. The system did not endure because the proceeds of the assigned revenues did not rise as fast as the expenditure of local authorities and because successive

Governments were unwilling to increase the range or percentage of the revenues paid to the Local Taxation Account. Although a failure, the assigned revenue idea is of much significance. It was an attempt to isolate central aid to local government from other types of national expenditure and thereby to reduce central supervision of local administration. It was also the start of a continuing argument about the relative desirability of general grants to local authorities as opposed to grants for specified purposes—a controversy examined more fully in Chapter V.

As noted above, the reform of the small units of government in county areas was delayed until 1894. The urban and rural sanitary districts became urban and rural district councils of the pre-1974 model. In urban areas the change was little more than one of name. In rural areas the effect was more complex because the Local Government Act, 1894, provided that a rural district area should not overlap a county boundary. Since the rural sanitary areas were based on the poor law unions which ignored county divisions, some reshaping of authorities was required. Rural districts acquired the duties of the rural sanitary districts, the highway responsibilities of the parish or those of the highway districts where such existed. The relationship with the Poor Law Guardians was reversed. Previously the powers of the rural sanitary district were exercised by those Guardians representing rural parishes: after 1894 the rural district councillors also served as members of the Board of Guardians. The parishes were also overhauled and given, like the districts, a ratepayer franchise. However, the powers of the parish had largely been transferred to larger authorities. Some parishes were too small to justify the creation of a council: the Act decreed that parishes with 300 inhabitants must have a council, those with less than 100 could not, and those between 100 and 300 could choose. In the absence of a parish council, parish business has to be transacted at a parish meeting. London was left untouched in 1894. This final remnant of eighteenth-century chaos was removed by the London Government Act, 1899, which replaced a miscellany of district boards and parish authorities in the LCC area by 28 Metropolitan Borough Councils, which were thought of as a counter-weight to the LCC which the Conservative Government feared might become too powerful—a suspicion aggravated by what appeared to be its permanent Radical majority. Although the Metropolitan Boroughs were given responsibility for public health, housing, rating, libraries and recreational services, they never achieved parity of importance with the LCC. Due to the centralising tendency of modern times, as new duties were bestowed on local authorities they tended to go to the top tier, the LCC.

The passage of the London Government Act, 1899, completed a

new pattern of multi-purpose authorities elected on a ratepayer franchise. The complete system can be illustrated by a simple diagram.

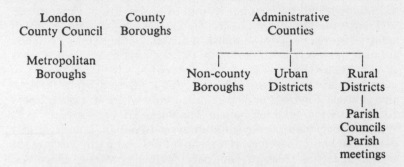

This structure remained until a fresh reform of London government took place in 1963.

Looking back over the nineteenth century it can be seen that it witnessed a constitutional revolution in local government. The Public Bill steadily replaced the Private Bill as the main instrument of change. A reconstructed system of elected, multi-purpose authorities emerged; the *ad hoc* principle went out of fashion. Separate organisations each devoted to a particular function have advantages. They can have areas most suitable for their particular purpose; they can generate specialised enthusiasm; they are not distracted by other tasks. However, the drawbacks of *ad hoc* bodies are substantial. They create a complex jumble of administrative units that is highly confusing for the public; if they are representative, the result must be a multiplicity of elections; the necessary co-ordination between them is difficult or impossible to arrange; either they cover a wide area and become remote or they are too small to use skilled manpower economically. Since the later Victorians were keener than we are now to uphold the representative principle, the move towards multi-purpose local authorities was wholly logical.

The intellectual forces advocating reform were powerful but not homogeneous. Sometimes they came in conflict with each other: this is one reason why the pace of change varied. The interaction of these ideas provides some explanation for the pattern of events and requires some attention.

The eighteen-thirties and forties were dominated by utilitarianism, the creed spread by Jeremy Bentham and his disciple James Mill. They argued that human affairs should be so organised as to secure the greatest happiness of the greatest number, that institutions should be judged by their utility, i.e. by the extent to which they contributed to the sum of happiness. This is not the place to examine the philosophical and moral limitations of the utilitarian view: a study of local government must be concerned with its consequences. It was essentially a radical doctrine. It implied that existing arrangements and institutions should not be accepted unless they satisfied the test of utility. The chaos of local administration was so complete that patently it failed the test. But utilitarianism did not require a wide extension of the functions of the state. On the contrary Bentham tended to accept the principle of *laissez-faire*—that the government should leave things alone. State action was required only where it was necessary to increase the total of human happiness—if it produced more pleasure than pain. Today utilitarianism is out of fashion, partly because it is unsatisfactory in terms of ethics and partly because the measurement of pleasure and pain presents obvious difficulties. Nevertheless Bentham probably has a greater effect on contemporary thought and action than is commonly admitted. Of course, the concepts have evolved. Utility has been replaced by efficiency. Instead of a calculus of pleasure and pain, the modern calculus is of cost and benefit which can be measured, or estimated, at least in monetary terms.

Another influential concept was representative government. This idea has a long history. It had a great impact at the time of the English Civil War. In the eighteenth century the American colonists revolted over the principle 'no taxation without representation'. Any claim for representation raises immediate practical questions—who should be represented and how should their representation be organised? Throughout the nineteenth century an increasing number of public bodies were elected and the franchise was extended; in the early years voting was restricted to some ratepayers and the number of votes each enjoyed might vary from one to six depending on the rateable value of their property, but by the end of the period each ratepayer had one vote. So there was progress towards a ratepayer democracy. But those who urged the need for representative government were not necessarily favourable to democracy. It was widely accepted that those who contributed to the local rate should control the spending of the money raised. John Stuart Mill, the son of James Mill, argued convincingly that participation in the process of government was a valuable education in public affairs which helped to produce a sense of responsibility in the community and stimulated the creation of local leadership. Yet to give the vote to all implied that policy might be controlled by the wishes of uneducated people— and of people who contributed little or nothing to the rates but derive benefit therefrom. However, the franchise for both parliamentary and local elections was steadily widened, partly because any limit appeared arbitrary and was awkward to defend politically, partly through the rise in educational standards and partly because limitation of the franchise caused administrative difficulties.

Utilitarian philosophy and demands for representative government reinforced each other in national politics. At local level they tended to come into conflict, at least before 1861. Chadwick regarded local self-government as potentially a vehicle for corruption. Utilitarianism demanded some element of central supervision of local administration to ensure that it was adequate and competent. The claim that the ratepayers, or their elected representatives, should decide how much to spend and how to spend it could easily clash with attempts to impose national standards. Controversy of this nature was widespread in connection with the development of drainage and other environmental health services. And the wider the representation, the greater the proportion of the populace to have the vote, the more likely were such clashes to arise: the poorer classes were more willing to take their chance of cholera and other diseases if this meant paying less in local rates. Opposition to central control led to the break up of the Central Board of Health in 1858. However, John Stuart Mill's *Representative Government* published in 1861 modified utilitarian doctrine in that it accepted the need to work with and through educated local opinion.

The third powerful force in local government was a feeling of humanity. This is an ageless sentiment; throughout time there has been some compassion for the poor, the ailing and the disabled. In a period when the Christian religion achieved great strength, one would expect humanity to influence public policy. However, it easily comes into conflict with other principles and baser motives. The administration of the poor law provides a clear example. Utilitarianism required a rigid, controlled and harsh regime to reduce cost, to stimulate self-help, in order to produce the greatest happiness for the greatest number. A humanitarian approach needed more flexibility, more charity and more expenditure. The reform of the poor law in 1834 was a triumph for utilitarian principles but slowly these were softened by slightly more generous administration.

Humanitarian thought stressed the dignity of the individual. It believed, to use a Victorian phrase, that people should be encouraged to better themselves. The argument can be presented with varying emphasis and degrees of sophistication. It is better for the country as a whole if everyone works hard to improve their position. God has given to each individual certain potentialities—it is therefore appropriate that these potentialities be used to the full. The same view can also be put without reference to God. Thus a climate of opinion was created favourable to state assistance to education, an attitude powerfully supported by the obvious need for a more highly skilled work force in an economy based on industrial processes of growing complexity.

Agreement that the state should take steps to promote human welfare necessarily required an erosion of support for *laissez-faire*. This doctrine, widely accepted in the early years of the century, argued that material prosperity was obtainable most speedily by fostering the spirit of free competition and leaving every man to work for his own interests. The role of the state, on this view, was minimal, limited to the preservation of internal order and security from external attack, and perhaps to provide bare essentials of life for those manifestly too weak to enter into the mêlée to acquire higher standards of comfort. But *laissez-faire* had no convincing solution to the problem of poverty caused through unemployment, to problems of public health or illiteracy. Even on questions of economic organisation it could not apply to the provision of services which required a heavy initial capital outlay and much interference with public and private rights. Free competition between railway companies, tramways, water and gas companies was obviously wasteful and undesirable. If price competition forced down standards of maintenance of equipment, the result was public danger. So the Victorians came to accept that there were natural monopolies that had to be controlled by the state, or provided by public authorities, to prevent exploitation of the consumer. Thus many towns provided their own water and gas supplies and later in the century electricity and tramways were added to the list of municipal trading services.

Support for representative institutions and humanitarian and utilitarian principles provided the driving force for change. But powerful pressures also worked against reform and hindered progress. Essentially these were the spirit of conservatism and the inevitable unpopularity of raising more money through taxation. These generalisations apply both to the nineteenth century and to our own time. It is easy to argue that things should be left as they are; that proposed changes are fraught with hidden difficulties; that the benefit of reform is exaggerated in relation to its cost. These attitudes will be promoted by wealthy persons and those in positions of authority who feel themselves threatened by change. Sometimes these established interests—Bentham called them sinister interests—have been so powerful as to be able to frustrate demands for reform: the history of the City of London in the nineteenth century is a paramount example of this situation.

TWENTIETH-CENTURY DEVELOPMENT OF SERVICES

The present century has seen a vast growth in the scale of services provided by local authorities. This has been accompanied by an increase in financial aid from the national Exchequer and an increase in supervision by central departments over local administration. The structural changes have been less impressive, and have failed to keep pace with the development of functions.

It is possible to summarise the structural alterations fairly briefly. The two major *ad hoc* authorities, the School Boards and the Boards of Guardians, came to an end in 1902 and 1930 respectively, the greater part of their duties being transferred to county boroughs and county councils. A number of towns achieved county borough status before 1926, when the population qualification was raised to 75,000 and the obstacle to this promotion was made more difficult by changing it from Provisional Order procedure to a Private Bill: between 1926 and 1964 only one new county borough was created. As the larger towns expanded, their suburbs overspilled their boundaries; by agreement between the councils concerned there were a large number of adjustments to county borough boundaries which substantially increased their population, acreage and rateable value. A number of urban districts obtained borough charters and thus achieved added civic dignity, if only very few extra powers. The areas of urban and rural districts (but not the non-county boroughs) were also rationalised in the nineteen-thirties by the reviews carried out by county councils under the provisions of the Local Government Act, 1929. As a result of these county reviews the total of urban districts was reduced from 786 to 573 and that of rural districts from 650 to 477. The policy of the counties varied. Rutland and Radnor, the two smallest counties, were excused by the Minister of Health from making any review at all. Other small counties undertook reviews but left the number of district authorities unchanged—e.g. Huntingdonshire and Flintshire. In some large counties, like Devon and Somerset, the review was also notably ineffective. Elsewhere, as in Cumberland and Northumberland, the county pruned out the tiny urban authorities but left the rural councils virtually untouched. Other counties followed the reverse policy, Northamptonshire and Shropshire amalgamated rural districts and left the urban councils alone. Finally, some counties, e.g. East Sussex and Hampshire, took strong action in both urban and rural districts. The greatest concentration of small districts was in Wales. Essentially this is because the Welsh counties enforced a minimum amount of change, but in areas of sparse population it can be argued that lower population figures for rural districts are essential otherwise their areas will become inconveniently large.

While the total amount of change has not been inconsiderable, the constitutional framework established in 1888 and 1894 remained basically the same until 1972. London is the exception. The London Government Act, 1963, pushed the metropolitan boundary out to embrace most of its suburbia and redefined the distribution of responsibilities between the upper and lower-tier authorities. There has been almost continuous discussion since the last war of the need to redesign the local government system: the various schemes of reform are examined in the following sections of this chapter.

To revert to the growth of services—the first big move forward in this century came in the field of education. In 1900 the school leaving age was raised from 12 to 14. This created an immediate difficulty. The School Boards had been given powers solely to provide elementary education: if 'elementary' was defined as being limited to the basic skills of reading, writing and arithmetic, then children of ability aged 12 and 13 would simply waste their time at the Board schools. Many of these schools started to provide more advanced instruction. In 1901 the Cockerton judgement held that the London School Board had no legal right to give advanced courses and provoked a crisis that demanded immediate action. The Education Act, 1902, abolished the 2,500 School Boards and transferred their responsibilities to the multi-purpose authorities. County councils and county boroughs were empowered to provide elementary and secondary education, but non-county boroughs with 10,000 population and urban districts with 20,000 population were made responsible for elementary education. Here is a principle that has not been widely used in local government—that the powers of an authority depend not only upon its status but also on its population. Since there was no arrangement for towns which subsequently achieved these population limits to acquire powers over elementary education, the result became anomalous: by the nineteen-thirties many boroughs and urban districts had grown rapidly and had no education powers although they were significantly larger than many authorities with these powers. The Education Act, 1944, concentrated education in the hands of counties and county boroughs, with the stipulation that limited powers should be delegated by county councils, especially to towns with a population above 60,000. Since 1944 the school leaving age has been raised to 16 and there has been a truly enormous expansion of further and technical education. There has to be increasing co-operation between local education authorities over the organisation of advanced courses in order to prevent wasteful duplication.

The abolition of the Poor Law Guardians was recommended in the 1909 Report of the Royal Commission on the Poor Law. The Report revealed wide disparities in poor law administration. Many of the Boards gave out-door relief with varying generosity and provided medical services for those who could not fairly be described as paupers. This policy was defensible on both humanitarian and economic grounds: if the working population had medical attention and kept healthy, they were less likely to become a burden on the poor rate. The Royal Commission's Report was not unanimous because a Minority Report urged more drastic remedial action to remove the stigma of poverty and to break up poor law administration by dividing education and health aspects from the relief of poverty. The Liberal Government introduced old age pensions and compulsory health insurance and so eased the Guardians' task. Yet no action was taken to transfer the Guardians' duties to the major local authorities, perhaps because the Cabinet was immersed in many other violent controversies, perhaps because of reluctance to entrust the poor to county councils largely dominated by Tory landowners. It is also true, as was stressed by the Minority Report, that many Guardians had carried out their unpopular task with humanity and imagination. So the Guardians survived for twenty years more. In the nineteen-twenties more Unions were controlled by Labour majorities; these were accused by their opponents of extravagant expenditure. The Poplar Guardians led by George Lansbury at one stage refused to pay their share of the expenditure of the London County Council owing to the high cost of poor relief in Poplar. Allegations of corruption by the Guardians were widespread. An Act passed in 1926 gave the Minister of Health power to take over the duties of the Guardians if he found their administration to be defective: this was done in three places, Bedwellty, Chester-le-Street and West Ham. Ultimately the Guardians disappeared in 1930 under the terms of the Local Government Act passed the previous year. Their duties were taken over by the county councils and county boroughs and divided up between committees dealing with health, education and public assistance. The latter function was transferred to central government agencies in two stages with the establishment of the Unemployment Assistance Board in 1934 and the National Assistance Board in 1948. Also in 1948 came the final break up of the poor law when the Children Act and the National Assistance Act redefined the powers of counties and county boroughs to care for children, the aged and the infirm.

Personal health services remained in an administrative tangle until 1964. Hospitals had three origins—voluntary organisations, the Boards of Guardians and public health authorities. The Guardians were concerned with medical services for the poor while the health authorities were required to isolate persons suffering from infectious disease. After 1930 the medical wards of workhouses were taken over by the health committees of the counties and county boroughs and turned into general purpose hospitals. County boroughs, counties, and some other boroughs and urban districts were made responsible for maternity and child welfare from 1907 onwards and had opened clinics for this purpose. The National Health Service Act, 1946, transferred all hospitals to the new Regional Hospital Boards, but an expanded range of medical duties, including the aftercare of hospital patients, the provision of health visitors and home helps was allocated to counties and county boroughs.

The construction of council houses and flats was started before the end of the nineteenth century. It was then thought of as an aspect of public health because the slums were breeding-places for disease and their progressive replacement was a medical requirement. After the First World War the public provision of housing was accepted as a social need, and various Acts were passed which gave national financial assistance towards council building. Housing powers went to the boroughs, urban and rural district councils. This is the one modern service not allocated to county councils. Indeed, without the housing function it is difficult to see how many district councils could now justify their existence.

In the nineteen-twenties there was a great rise in the popularity of motoring. The increase in traffic created demands for higher standards of road maintenance. It will be remembered that highways were then the responsibility of the boroughs and districts, save that the counties maintained the more important 'county' roads. The Local Government Act, 1929, sought to improve the state of the roads in the countryside by transferring the powers of rural districts to the county councils. Towns with a population above 20,000 were allowed to 'claim' highway powers over county roads within their boundaries and all urban authorities remained responsible for minor roads. Rural districts and towns below 20,000 could also be given delegated powers over county roads, but this sort of delegation was never very important or satisfactory and has been steadily reduced. Care of roads demands highly skilled supervision and equipment which becomes more complex and expensive: here the case for centralisation of responsibility is strong on economic and technical grounds.

Town and country planning is a further example of the transfer of functions to the higher tier of local authorities. All the earliest planning legislation from 1909 to 1932 had given boroughs and districts the opportunity to introduce local planning schemes. But this multiplicity of planning authorities proved a serious hindrance to the effective control of development—there were, for example, 133 planning authorities in the area served by London Transport. In fact, only a small part of the country had been covered by operative planning schemes prepared by borough and district councils, partly because of the intricate procedure and also due to fear of liability to pay compensation. The Town and Country Planning Act, 1947, centralised responsibility in the hands of counties and county boroughs and introduced a comprehensive system for the control of development. Again, there were also limited powers for counties to delegate decisions to non-county boroughs and district councils.

The police and the fire brigade provide further examples of the transfer of functions to fewer and larger units of operation. After the Police Act, 1946, the remaining non-county borough forces were absorbed into the county police; in the nineteen-sixties the centralisation process continued with the amalgamation of county and county borough forces. Counties became the fire authority under the Fire Brigades Act, 1947. Other powers have been taken away from local authorities altogether. This started with the creation of Regional Traffic Commissioners in 1930 and the loss to them of the power to license road passenger services. Relief of the unemployed went to the Unemployment Assistance Board in 1934. In the post-war period gas and electricity undertakings were nationalised and hospitals were taken over by regional boards. The loss of powers continued with the transfer to *ad hoc* authorities in 1974 of personal health services, water supply and sewerage.

For a century after the reform of the poor law in 1834 local authorities enjoyed a steady growth of their responsibilities. In the post-war period while some further powers have been obtained, others have been taken away. Increasingly, the losses outweigh the gains. Local government is in competition with other types of public body. It faces the challenge of rival institutions.

How can this change of fortune be explained? There were two main reasons for the burgeoning of local government after 1834. The agreement that public provision of services should be allowed to develop was a hesitant agreement, for this period was the heyday of individualistic doctrines. The sentiment that government of any kind is but a necessary evil leads also to the supposition that local government is a lesser evil than national government because it is more susceptible to public control. The great indignation aroused by the attempts of national government to influence local affairs in the Chadwick period is eloquent proof of the force of this attitude. The second reason can be stated quite simply—local government had no competitors. The highly competent Civil Service of today evolved very slowly in the latter part of the nineteenth century. Even in the early years of this century the organisational resources of government departments were rudimentary except for tax collection. Public corporations did not appear until the nineteen-twenties. Thus the administrative capacity of local authorities, however deficient it may have been by modern standards, held a dominating position.

All this has now changed. Collectivism is in fashion rather than individualism: technical requirements demand large-scale production to achieve economies of scale: the need for efficiency and uniformity is held to require fewer and bigger units of organisation. Take the particular example of the health service. There was an undeniable case for bringing together under one management the three original sections of the National Health Service—the personal health services provided by local authorities, the hospitals and the various individual practitioners. Why could they not be unified within the context of a democratically controlled local government system? The traditional objection, that local authority areas are unsuitable, might have been met if the needs of the health service had been taken into account when local government areas were reshaped in 1972. However, there were three other powerful factors working against the claims of local government. The professional interests involved, particularly the doctors, feared the loss of freedom if they were subject to the direction of local councillors. Local authorities have inadequate financial resources to provide all health services; they would require either new powers to tax or massive additional grants from the central government. And if national government money is being spent, then Ministers like to be able to control how it is done. There is no doubt that the reluctance of many local authorities to provide family planning facilities has aroused irritation in Whitehall.

Thus local government is on the defensive. In any discussion about how a new service should be provided, or how some existing service could be reformed, the case for local government no longer dominates; on the contrary, it is increasingly difficult to sustain.

Chapter II

PROPOSALS FOR REFORM 1945-72

THE NEED FOR CHANGE

The patterns of economic and social affairs in Great Britain steadily become more uniform. The process can be traced back through the centuries but has been more pronounced in recent years. Technological progress has improved communications so distance matters less and less. It is much easier to administer large areas. The mass media aid public knowledge of what happens in other places. A better educated and more articulate public opinion tends to demand equality of treatment; if certain facilities are available in another county or another city, why are they not available here? This kind of pressure helps to involve the national political parties more deeply in local issues. Meanwhile the growth of local services has been so substantial that their total cost has a major impact on national resources. So the Cabinet of whatever party wants to try and steer local authorities towards policies that will not conflict with their own programme.

All these tendencies point towards a more centralised system of local government with fewer and larger local authorities. If uniformity is more highly regarded than local initiative, then less stress will be placed on the need to encourage local representation. Yet this line of thought conflicts totally with the philosophy on which the pre-1974 structure of local government was based. Its foundation was three Acts of Parliament passed at the end of the nineteenth century which were designed to ensure that local councils responded to the wishes of local ratepayers. Late Victorians insisted on ratepayer democracy. In geographical terms they commonly utilised boundaries which already existed, including county boundaries which can be traced back to feudal times. The structure as it stood in 1972 had been created in a different age for the needs of a different age, when the duties of local authorities were far more limited and before the internal combustion engine had revolutionised means of transport. Prior to 1972 little had been done to modernise the Victorian legacy. True there had been some changes. Between 1888 and 1929 just over 20 new county boroughs were created; in the nineteen-thirties the number of county districts was substantially reduced; boundaries of boroughs were widened to embrace advancing suburbia; some urban districts achieved the dignity of borough status and so became able to parade a mayor and aldermen on ceremonial occasions. But the pace of change has been slowed down by the clash of local interests, particularly between counties and boroughs. The counties managed to prevent the establishment of any new county boroughs between 1929 and 1964, motivated by the fear that new county boroughs would mean loss of some rateable value by the counties.

Thus the local government map failed to adjust to movements and growth of population. Anomalies inherited from the Victorians became more glaring while others emerged. In 1972 the largest administrative county, Lancashire, had a population over one hundred times greater than that of the smallest county, Radnor, and over eighty times greater than that of Rutland, the smallest English county. In the county borough class, Birmingham was thirty times the size of Canterbury. There were also second-tier authorities with a population three times that of Canterbury. Over 30 county districts, most of them in Wales, had less than 2,000 inhabitants. It was even possible to find third-tier authorities, suburbanised parishes in rural districts, with a population not far short of that of Radnor.

The existence of many small county districts had a profound effect on the allocation of local government duties. Legislation has assumed, with minor exceptions, e.g. libraries, that all local authorities of any one type must be given equal statutory rights in respect of any function. It was also held that functions cannot be subdivided, so that if a county must be given a particular part of a function, like education, it must have the whole of it. Yet highways were a notable exception to this rule. But the total effect was to drain functions away from the second-tier authorities and to change the pattern of local administration not by a comprehensive scheme of reform but by *ad hoc* measures relating to individual functions. Thus the second-tier authorities lost powers over elementary education, planning, fire service, personal health services and rural roads to the county councils. This aggravated tensions between counties and the larger county districts and led to demands for the delegation of county responsibilities to the larger districts—a clumsy compromise that often worked badly.

Another outdated concept that stayed until the 1972 Act was the differentiation between urban and rural districts. Nineteenth-century legislation was based on the belief that the countryside needed fewer services than the towns, notably in relation to sewerage. Subsequently the difference in powers between urban and rural districts was often reduced, but twin organisations with virtually identical tasks were often located in the same small town where an urban district or borough served an inner area and was divided by an antique boundary from the rural district serving the hinterland.

The main failing of the pre-1972 system, however, was that many of the top-tier units were too small. Specialised services which demand the use of highly qualified staff, purpose-built accommodation and expensive equipment can only be provided economically for a substantial population. Planning also cannot be carried out effectively except over wide areas. The minimum size for top-tier units has been a matter of constant argument, but estimates continually increased. In 1888 the minimum population for county borough status was 50,000 and four exceptions below that figure were permitted. In 1926 the minimum was raised to 75,000; in 1958 to 100,000. Evidence given by government departments to the Redcliffe-Maud Commission was thinking in terms of 200–300,000 while the County Councils Association envisaged half a million. Government departments are attracted by the idea of fewer and larger local authorities as being easier to supervise in the interests of uniformity. Local authorities slowly accepted the need for bigger units out of fear that they would lose functions to other sectors of public administration.

If the case for change was so strong—one may well ask why so much time elapsed before any effective reforms were achieved? What were the obstacles? Reformers commonly fail to appreciate the extent and value of local patriotism. Councillors who had given much devoted service to a local authority could not be expected to welcome its demise and tended to resent any implication that their council had not been efficient. Local government officers, especially chief officers, feared the effect of change on their personal status. Ratepayers often feared, without firm evidence, that proposed alterations would adversely affect the local rates. Behind these forces of local opinion stood the national pressure groups, the associations of local authorities, always ready to try to safeguard the interests of their members. Inevitably the different types of authority, notably counties and county boroughs, had opposing ideas as to the optimum pattern for local government. Successive Governments have been weak in being unwilling to enforce basic alterations in the absence of a general consensus among the interested parties. Politically reform of local government was an awkward topic. Many councillors are leading local personalities well able to make their views known to a local MP, and faced with sufficiently strong and influential local pressure a Government backbench MP might even find it expedient to ignore the party whip in the House of Commons on this issue. And there is a great difference between accepting the need for reform in principle and accepting a particular scheme which would drastically upset the established arrangements for representation and administration in your own area.

A VARIETY OF IDEAS

During the last war, considerable interest developed in the need for local government reform. In part, this was an aspect of the nation-wide discussion on post-war reconstruction; in part it was stimulated because the existing structure of authorities was seen to be ill-adapted to meet the emergencies of war. Various plans were put forward, e.g. by the Labour Party, the Association of Municipal Corporations and NALGO, each of which recognised the need for larger areas of administration for some purposes. These reports now belong to the history of local government but they helped to create a climate of opinion which caused the Government to take action.

Almost the last measure of the war-time coalition Cabinet was to promote the Local Government (Boundary Commission) Act, 1945, which established a Boundary Commission authorised to propose limited changes outside London. The limitations were all important, for the Commission was given no power over functions, so it could not introduce any new *type* of authority. Any prospect of regional government was eliminated from the start. (Local authorities were very hostile to the regional concept because of their dealings with the war-time Regional Commissioners.) Also excluded was any new arrangement to deal with the special problems of conurbations. The Commission had to work within the traditional model of local government: it could divide and amalgamate counties, demote county boroughs, create new ones, or amalgamate and divide them, and change the geographical arrangement of second-tier authorities. The Commission studied their problem for over two years, then reported that their powers were insufficient to initiate the changes needed and set out the details of a wholly new structure. One-tier local government was to be kept in only 17 of the largest cities with a minimum population of 200,000, to be known as one-tier counties. The remainder of the country, including the Lancashire-Cheshire conurbations, was to have a two-tier system. The major authorities would be reshaped counties, again with a minimum population of 200,000, so that the smaller counties would be amalgamated and in a few cases the largest counties would be subdivided. Within these counties would be boroughs and urban and rural districts, together with a new type of authority confusingly termed 'county boroughs' which would exercise all powers except for planning, police, fire service and main roads. The new county boroughs would be Liverpool, Manchester and other towns in the population bracket 60,000–200,000. Thus there were to be three categories of town, one-tier counties, county boroughs and other boroughs: this plan had the advantage of easing the sharp contrast in status between the wholly independent county boroughs and other urban authorities.

The changes proposed were far too sweeping to be easily acceptable and in 1949 the Boundary Commission was dissolved and its ideas were consigned unloved to civil service archives.

The issue then remained dormant until 1953 when the Conservative Government asked the associations of local authorities to re-examine the problem. It seemed that the Government hoped that the associations might arrive at an agreed set of principles that could provide the basis for reform. The hope was delusory. The associations produced two conflicting schemes for reform and it was clear that there could be no agreement on principles for fundamental change. The only way in which the Government could gain broad consent from the associations was to propose a scheme which would lead to relatively minor adjustments in the existing structure.

The Local Government Act, 1958, thereupon established two fresh Boundary Commissions, one for England and one for Wales. The Commissions were instructed to carry out their tasks within the present framework of county and county borough organisation. Thus they could propose the creation or amalgamation or demotion of county boroughs; they could suggest boundary adjustments between top-tier authorities. The English Commission had wider powers in the conurbations (described in the 1958 Act as the special review areas of Tyneside, West Yorkshire, South-East Lancashire, Merseyside and the West Midlands) where it could propose the establishment of a 'continuous county' in which the distribution of functions between the county and the second-tier authorities might depart from the normal pattern. The English Commission divided the country into areas and studied them piecemeal. As a start, the Commission held preliminary consultations with local authorities and then issued draft proposals. Before changes could take place, there was a long road to travel. The procedure designed for consultations, enquiries and appeals was so complex that some five years elapsed between the start of local discussions and the operative date for any actual changes. Plenty of opportunity was given for public opinion to make itself felt; the force of opinion might cause a Commission to change its mind or lead the Minister to reject the final plans of a Commission. There was a marked tendency for each stage of decision-making to reduce the amount of change.

A number of factors led to the decline of the English Commission. Wales is considered separately below. The morass of procedure for dealing with objectors strangled any impetus in its work. Some of its schemes seemed to be designed to arouse a maximum of ill-feeling while achieving a minimum of benefit. Does it really matter whether Lyme Regis is in Dorset or Devon? The Commission would have proceeded more speedily and probably with more influence had it concentrated always on major issues. But on major issues the Commission got little support from the Government. The reprieve of Rutland was the most glaring example. With only 25,000 people Rutland was forced to rely heavily on its neighbours to assist in the provision of services. After Rutland the Commission lost credibility.

The final death blow to the Commission, and perhaps it was a happy release, came from the appointment of a Minister of Housing and Local Government, Mr Richard Crossman, who was determined to accomplish radical reforms. A few sentences of his address to the 1965 Conference of the Association of Municipal Corporations at Torquay are worth quoting. He argued that '. . . the whole structure of local government is out of date, that our county borough and county councils as at present organised are archaic institutions whose size and structure make them increasingly ill-adapted to fulfilling the immensely important functions with which they are charged. The greatest obstacle, in fact, which prevents efficient councils from retaining public confidence is the obsolete constitutional framework within which they had to operate.' From a responsible Minister these were striking words. After some further delay the English Commission was wound up in 1966 and was replaced by a Royal Commission which could examine the whole subject afresh and with a clean sheet.

In contrast with their hesitant action in the provinces the Conservative Government took a much firmer line over the reform of London government. One reason was that action in London imposed virtually no strain on party loyalties. As the London County Council was commonly dominated by a Labour majority, a Conservative Cabinet had few political inhibitions about promoting change. In 1957 a Royal Commission had been established to study the special characteristics of the capital and the surrounding area which, therefore, was excluded from the operations of the English Commission established by the 1958 Act. The central difficulty in London was the absence of any local authority which embraced the whole of the built-up zone. The London County Council had inherited the 1855 boundary of the Metropolitan Board of Works which a century later had ceased to have any connection with geographical realities. London spilled over into large sections of Kent, Surrey, Hertfordshire, Essex and the whole of Middlesex. Little more than a third of the population of Greater London lived within the LCC area, and the LCC population of 3,200,000 was still declining slowly. There were also three county boroughs in Greater London—Croydon, East Ham and West Ham—so nine top-tier authorities in the London area were each responsible for broad issues of planning policy. No single local authority could have a synoptic view of the issues connected with the redevelopment and zoning of Greater London, the movement of population and the construction of main traffic arteries.

In brief outline this was the situation facing the Royal Commission on London Government. Its Report, Cmnd 1164 of 1960, unanimously urged drastic changes. The Commission was of opinion that a Council for Greater London should be established to be responsible for overall planning, main roads, fire and ambulance services. It would also share responsibility for education, housing, planning applications and certain other services with a new type of second-tier authority—Greater London Boroughs. These Greater London Boroughs would have the status and constitution of municipal boroughs except that the City of London would be permitted to retain its ancient institutions. The Commission's scheme envisaged 52 of these Boroughs with populations between 100,000 and 250,000 —except, again, for the City of London: they would be responsible for health and welfare services, child care, local roads and libraries, in addition to the duties shared with the Council for Greater London. Reorganisation on this scale involved the disappearance of the LCC, Middlesex and three county boroughs, substantial loss of territory and rateable value by four county councils, and extensive amalgamations of county districts and Metropolitan Boroughs. These proposals aroused considerable opposition in the Labour Party and also in some suburban fringe areas which heartily disliked the prospect of integration with the metropolis.

In this instance, however, the Government were not deflected by local hostility. They accepted the broad lines of the Royal Commission's Report and the London Government Act, 1963, now provides an opportunity for the co-ordinated planning of the whole metropolitan area. There were some modifications to the Commission's proposals. The number of London Boroughs was reduced from 52 to 32. There were two reasons for this change: first, some fringe areas were excluded from the London area altogether and remain in Surrey and Essex; and second, and far more important, the minimum population of London Boroughs was doubled. This rise to 200,000 was due partly to the further decision that London Boroughs shall have full powers over education—save in the former LCC territory where a committee of the GLC, the Inner London Education Authority, representing the area concerned, has this responsibility.

To return to the problems of provincial England, the Royal Commission was appointed in February, 1966, under the Chairmanship of Lord Redcliffe-Maud with these terms of reference:

'To consider the structure of local government in England, outside Greater London, in relation to its existing functions; and to make recommendations for authorities and boundaries, and for functions and their division, having regard to the size and the character of areas in which these can be most effectively exercised and the need to sustain a viable system of democracy.'

It will be noted that this phraseology contains a hint of the perennial conflict between efficiency and democracy. The choice of chairman was also significant: one expected Lord Redcliffe-Maud to produce a structure in harmony with the ideas of the earlier Maud Committee on the internal management of local authorities which showed a heavy emphasis on efficiency.

The views of government departments presented to the Commission showed quite remarkable similarity. All favoured larger units of local government in the interests of efficiency and uniformity. No doubt they felt that fewer local authorities would be easier to supervise. The Ministry of Transport wished for 30–40 major transport authorities to replace the then 823 highway authorities and 1,190 parking authorities. Indeed, all departments favoured 30–40 major authorities. How did these magic figures occur separately to so many minds? Within the overall figure of 30–40 authorities there was some variation of approach. Education sought a population of 500,000 with a minimum of 300,000, but Health was prepared to go down to 200,000. There was also difference about the need for second-tier authorities: Housing and Local Government accepted the need for a second-tier, the Treasury assumed all-purpose authorities while Transport was unsure—'there is no advantage in creating lower-tier authorities in areas which could be adequately governed at first-tier level'.

The departmental view that education authorities required a population of 500,000 implied that the London Boroughs were far too small to be effective education authorities. This was curious since these authorities were created as recently as 1963, and minimum sizes of authority are generally thought of as being *higher* in densely populated areas. Further, the evidence submitted by the inspectorate in the Department of Education and Science indicated that the quality of service suffered where the population of an LEA was below 200,000: however, the inspectors judged authorities in the 200–250,000 bracket to be superior to those in the 300–400,000 bracket and equal to those in the 400–500,000 range. Thus the 500,000 standard and absolute minimum of 300,000 suggested by the Department were open to objection.

The Report of the Royal Commission (Cmnd 4040) was published in July 1969. It is impossible for a brief summary to do full justice to the Report and the Memorandum of Dissent by Mr Derek Senior. The Commission found six weaknesses in the local government system each of which are discussed elsewhere in this book; the six problems were the division between town and country, the division between county boroughs and counties, division of responsibility within counties, the small size of many authorities, the relationship between local authorities and the public and between local authorities and the central government. Obviously, these items were interrelated. The distinction between town and country, county and county borough, aggravated relations between central and local government because Ministers and civil servants had to deal with separate local authority associations. The minute size of some authorities tended to raise levels of central supervision over all councils. The division of functions between different types of authority was confusing to the public. Councils were often deeply concerned by problems that were the responsibility of another authority. This analysis pointed clearly to two solutions—bigger authorities and a greatly simplified system.

The Commission (except Mr Senior) therefore proposed that the greater part of England be divided into 58 unitary authorities which would be responsible for almost all executive action in relation to local government services. Unitary areas would embrace town and countryside. The major towns which provide a focus for the commerce and cultural life of the surrounding area should also constitute the centre for local government. The administrative map would be made to coincide as far as possible with contemporary economic and social geography. Inevitably, this concept fitted some parts of the country better than others. The population of the 58 units suggested by the Commission varied from 195,000 for the Halifax area to well over a million in Sheffield and South Yorkshire. The Report accepted that there would be serious disadvantages in terms of size and remoteness if the population of an all-purpose unitary authority was much more than a million. So a quite different two-tier system was proposed for the three largest conurbations; this was similar but not identical, to the pattern that has operated in London since 1963. In these three areas, the West Midlands, Merseyside and Selnec, i.e. South-East Lancashire and North-East Cheshire, the top-tier or metropolitan authority would have been responsible for planning, transportation, water supply, sewerage, refuse disposal, police, fire and ambulance services; some tasks were to be split between upper and lower tiers, notably housing and provision of entertainment and recreation facilities; all other duties would rest with the 20 lower-tier metropolitan districts. This plan would have given the districts a very important role with responsibility for personal services including education. The whole scheme involved a direct reversal of traditional wisdom about local government: it had been assumed that single-tier authorities were suitable for compact urban areas but that more sparsely populated rural areas required a multi-tier system. The Royal Commission argued that the single-tier arrangement is appropriate for mixed urban and rural areas while the two-tier system should be reserved for the greatest urban concentrations.

Set above the unitary and metropolitan authorities already described, the Commission recommended the establishment of eight provincial councils covering areas coinciding with those of the economic planning regions. Provincial bodies were to be largely recruited by indirect election, i.e. elected by the unitary and metropolitan authorities, and would co-opt between 20 per cent and 25 per cent of their membership. A quotation from the Commission's Report best describes their purpose, 'The (provincial) council's chief task will be to create a broad strategic framework for the exercise of main authorities' operational responsibilities.' Certainly this section of the Report was vague. It is hard to see how indirectly elected bodies can exercise dynamic influence. Provincial councils were intended to provide a link between local authorities and the central government; they could have become a means of helping to persuade local authorities to accept central government programmes and priorities. Not surprisingly this idea did not attract much support.

Other proposals from the Commission reflected the views of the Report of the Maud Committee on Management issued two years earlier. Aldermen should be abolished. No council should have more than 75 members. The number of committees should be small. A central committee should work out priorities. Every authority should appoint a chief executive, chosen regardless of professional background. Delegation to officers should be freely exercised. Local offices should be established where the public can seek advice.

The main issue facing the Commission was the choice between essentially one-tier and two-tier local government. Here a dispute arose between the Commission and one of their number, Mr Derek Senior. Mr Senior was a journalist specialising in local government and had committed himself, before appointment to the Commission, to the concept of 30–40 City Regions as being the optimum basis for local government reorganisation. It is arguable that anyone who is already committed to a particular solution to a problem is unsuitable to serve on a body designed to advise upon it. Not surprisingly, Mr Senior pursued his idea of a City Region and became estranged from his colleagues. There is some similarity between his City Region

concept and the unitary authorities since both ensure the amalgamation of town and country. But the 35 Senior City Regions were
larger: 20 of the 35 regions would have had virtually a million or
more inhabitants. All members of the Commission were agreed that
units of this size were too large to be all-purpose authorities and so the
Senior plan proposed 148 district councils. The Senior City Regions
would have been responsible for planning, transportation, water
supply, sewerage, police, fire, education and 'capital investment
programming': other more personal services would be left to the
district authorities. Mr Senior also proposed minor local common
councils and five indirectly elected provincial authorities. The differences between the Majority Report and the Senior dissent can be
illustrated by a diagram.

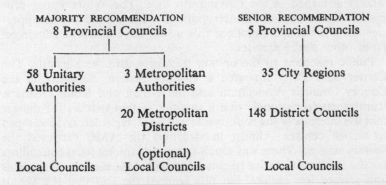

The crucial clash was over the principle of unitary authorities.
Thirty-five City Regions would certainly fit in well with the evidence
presented by government departments. Why then did the Commission
reject this plan? Essentially because the majority of members were
convinced of the value of all-purpose county borough type authorities: where responsibility for local government is undivided, then
co-operation between services is much easier. Since the Senior units
were too big to be all-purpose authorities, smaller units had to be
found. The Report noted that the evidence of the DES inspectors
did not support the Department's claim that an education authority
should have a population of half a million; Lord Redcliffe-Maud and
his colleagues were therefore prepared to accept unitary authorities
of 250,000 people, or even less in a few cases. They also tried, in
contrast to Senior, to respect existing local boundaries wherever
possible. The argument against unitary authorities is that it is
impossible to define areas which are suitable for the operation of all
local government services. One is forced to choose either areas

suitable for planning purposes which are too large and remote for personal services, or a framework suitable for personal services, that is too small for planning.

The views of the Labour Government on these problems were set out in a White Paper, *Reform of Local Government in England* (Cmnd 4276), published in February 1970. In general, the ideas of the majority of the Commission were accepted. However, two further areas were added to the two-tier metropolitan category— South Hampshire and West Yorkshire. This reduced unitary authorities from 58 to 51 and increased metropolitan areas from 3 to 5 and metropolitan districts from 20 to 28. In effect, seven unitary areas were demoted to metropolitan districts and an extra district was created for the Isle of Wight which previously would have been wholly absorbed in the Portsmouth unit. The White Paper proposed that education in metropolitan areas should be an upper-tier not a lower-tier function; this would have divorced education from other social services.

Public reactions to the unitary authority idea were hostile. The Conservative Party favoured a two-tier system. So also did the County Councils Association and the Urban and Rural Districts. Rural areas feel strongly that a two-tier system reduces the danger that the interests of the countryside will be disregarded and swamped by urban centres. Almost in isolation the AMC favoured the unitary scheme. There was much sympathy among local councillors for the Senior alternative because it provided for more local councils and seemed less remote, but this ignored the fact that the Senior scheme would have produced fewer and larger education authorities and that his proposed boundaries would do more to disturb present administrative and social patterns. All the pressure was for more representation, more 'democracy' and, in general, to water down the scale of reform. The election of a Conservative Government in 1970 ensured that the concept of unitary authorities was dead.

As a postscript to the discussion of proposals for structural reform, mention must be made of the separate developments in Wales. Here the local authorities, except in South Wales, tended to be weak in terms of population and rateable values. In spite of very considerable financial aid from the national Exchequer it had been difficult to maintain a standard of service comparable with that enjoyed in other areas. The 1958 Commission for Wales intended to deal with this situation by a drastic plan of county amalgamations which would have reduced the number of Welsh counties from thirteen to seven. Anglesey alone was to remain intact. Inevitably, the plan was hotly opposed in Wales. Local patriotism was incensed by the complete disregard of existing county boundaries and some of the new counties proposed were both large and inconvenient in shape. Inevitably these proposals were rejected. Subsequently an inter-departmental working party was established to review Welsh problems. Its conclusions, published in 1967, were that Merthyr Tydfil should cease to be a county borough and that the counties be reduced from thirteen to five by a process of amalgamation of whole units. Subsequently this number was raised to six when the Government agreed that North Wales should form two counties instead of one. The four new counties suggested were:

Clwyd   —a combination of Denbighshire and Flintshire.
Dyfed   —a combination of Cardiganshire, Carmarthenshire and Pembrokeshire.
Gwynedd—a combination of Anglesey, Caernarvonshire and Merionethshire.
Powys   —a combination of Breconshire, Montgomeryshire and Radnorshire.

Glamorgan and Monmouthshire, renamed Gwent, were to remain. Thus with the three remaining county boroughs, Cardiff, Newport and Swansea, there would have been nine major local authorities in Wales. At the second-tier level the proposal was to reduce the number of councils from 164 to 36.

No action was taken on these plans in spite of the wide measure of agreement to support them. The Redcliffe-Maud Report and the Labour Government's acceptance of unitary authorities for England injected a new element into the situation. If county boroughs were to disappear in England, then the retention of three 1888-style county boroughs in Wales became anomalous. So the Secretary of State for Wales announced a new plan in 1970 to create three Maud-type unitary authorities in South Wales, one for Newport and Monmouthshire, one for Cardiff and East Glamorgan and a third for Swansea and West Glamorgan. This would have reduced the number of major authorities in Wales to seven. The application of the unitary principle to South Wales caused a storm of protest, not least because it involved the dropping of district councils within the unitary areas. A fresh anomaly was created: in England, two-tier local government was to be restricted to the main centres of population, but in Wales it was to apply to the less populous areas, Clwyd, Dyfed, Gwynedd and Powys. This dilemma was also resolved by the election of a Conservative administration wedded to the concept of two-tier local government.

THE EMERGENCE OF THE 1972 ACT

The new Government in 1970 grasped the nettle of local government reform with commendable vigour. The Ministry of Housing and Local Government was renamed the Department of the Environment to stress the breadth of its responsibility to promote good living conditions. Early in 1969 a Commission on the Constitution had been appointed with wide terms of reference—'to consider the relations between the central government and the several countries, nations and regions of the United Kingdom'. Clearly, this broad inquiry would have provided a good excuse to postpone changes in the structure of local administration. The opportunity for delay was ignored. The new Secretary of State, Mr Peter Walker, moved ahead and quite rapidly prepared a fresh policy.

A White Paper published in February, 1971, *Local Government in England* (Cmnd 4584), argued that regional or provincial areas would be too large for the operation of local government services so that local government reorganisation could proceed independently of other changes that might be made subsequently in regional administration or representation. The White Paper itself was remarkably brief. A mere dozen pages outlined the basis of a new system of local government. The detailed geographical application of these principles was set out in a separate document, Department of the Environment Circular 8/71. The White Paper recognised the ever-competing claims of efficiency, which demanded larger units of organisation, and representative democracy which favoured smaller units. A fair compromise had to be made between them but where the arguments were evenly balanced the White Paper promised that the case for fuller representation would be decisive. So the tasks of local government were to be divided between two tiers of authorities, counties and districts. The allocation of functions was to differ between the main industrial areas with heavy concentrations of population and the remainder of England which is predominantly rural or semi-rural. Thus there are two styles of local government system, the metropolitan and the non-metropolitan.

The crucial distinction between the two lies in the distribution of responsibility for education, including libraries, and the personal social services. It was argued in the White Paper that the effective organisation of these functions required a population between 250,000 and one million, although these limits were not to be rigidly applied. The minimum figure was substantially below that advocated by the Department of Education and Science in its evidence to the Royal Commission. In the conurbations it is possible to form second-tier districts compact in size which fall within this population range. Here the districts can undertake education and the social services. Six metropolitan areas were proposed—Merseyside, Greater Manchester, West Midlands, West Yorkshire, South Yorkshire and

Tyneside. These metropolitan counties were to contain 34 metropolitan districts. The Conservative list of conurbations differed from
the Labour scheme issued a year before in that South Yorkshire and
Tyneside were added but South Hampshire was omitted.

In more rural areas the second-tier authorities must have a population far below 250,000 if they are to be reasonably small in area with
offices readily accessible for residents and councillors. Here the
major functions remain largely with the county council and the
distribution of powers between county and district remains very
similar to the previous pattern. The White Paper proposed the establishment of 38 non-metropolitan counties and the accompanying
DOE Circular outlined boundaries for the counties. Northumberland, the smallest non-metropolitan county in terms of population,
barely passed the 250,000 limit. At the other extreme six non-
metropolitan counties exceeded a million inhabitants. It is arguable
that the three largest, Essex, Hampshire and Kent, are too big to be
satisfactory representative bodies responsible for education and social
services, especially as they are all areas that can anticipate substantial
further growth in the immediate future. The DOE circular also
suggested boundaries for metropolitan districts. Here the population
range lay between 182,000 and 1,168,000 (Birmingham). It is notable
that many of these districts had a population and rateable resources
considerably below those of many demoted county boroughs. Clearly
the status of a local authority was to depend not only on size but
also on the nature of the area and its surroundings. A Boundary
Commission was established to delimit areas for non-metropolitan
districts and this body reported in 1972 with proposals for 278
districts with an average population around 100,000. As far as
possible the new district map was formed by amalgamations of
existing authorities. In the most remote rural areas district populations fall as low as 40,000. Largest districts are former county
boroughs which the Commission felt unable to split, e.g. Bristol, but
the fledgling county borough of Teesside was divided into three
districts. Subsequent negotiations secured some changes in the boundaries originally proposed, but in general, the original suggestions
were carried into effect.

The White Paper recognised the value of the third-tier authorities,
the rural parishes. These were to continue, but with powers rather
than duties. But what was to be done with the boroughs and urban
districts due to lose their separate identities in the reshaping of
second-tier authorities? Two solutions were offered. Either parish
councils could be established in essentially urban areas or local
communities might achieve some form of local representation through
non-statutory bodies, which might be assisted by district councils

financially or in other ways. Subsequently it was agreed that third-tier councils be formed in many of the former boroughs and urban districts within an upper population limit of approximately 20,000. Areas which had formed larger authorities were held not to need separate institutions as they would play a major role within the new district councils.

The practical effect of these changes was to vary greatly between different parts of England. In five shires, Cornwall, Hertfordshire, the Isle of Wight, Salop and Wiltshire, the only change was to district boundaries. Elsewhere there were adjustments to county boundaries and/or the amalgamation of former counties either in part or as a whole. Many of the new shires had to join with one or more former county boroughs, which, inevitably, resented their demotion. The shock was weaker where the county borough was already the geographical headquarters of the administrative county. Norwich and Nottingham were less disturbed than Plymouth, Portsmouth or Southampton. The complexity of reorganisation was greatest in the metropolitan areas because, apart from new boundaries, wholly new types of authority were to be created.

For Wales the proposals of the Conservative Government were in tune with their policy for England. The two-tier system was to prevail everywhere. The new pattern contained seven counties and 36 districts. Glamorgan was to be split into two and five other counties Clwyd, Dyfed, Gwent, Gwynedd and Powys were to be established broadly on the lines described above. The Local Government Act itself contained a further change: Glamorgan was divided into three sections. This further division is controversial because the new county of South Glamorgan is exceptional as it contains only two districts, one based on Cardiff and one on Barry. Cardiff dwarfs the remainder of the county. There are examples in England where a major city has a predominant position within a county but nowhere is this so overwhelming as in South Glamorgan. Whether Cardiff should have such exceptional treatment must be a matter of opinion.

The 1972 Act emerged after at least 25 years of intermittent official discussions about local government reform. Its passage to the statute book was relatively easy. The Labour Party opposed the Bill in Parliament, but the Party's position was weakened by its earlier acceptance of the unitary authority plan advocated by the majority of the Royal Commission, an idea that was widely unpopular. Nor did Labour's other main objections to the Bill arouse much enthusiasm. To urge that metropolitan counties rather than districts should be given responsibility for education was to move against the current of opinion demanding fuller representation and participation.

Another important criticism was that boundaries had been drawn too tightly around the metropolitan areas with the consequence that these authorities would find it difficult or impossible to obtain the land needed for housing development in the foreseeable future—at least within their own territory. Obviously the 'fringe' areas immediately affected did not share this attitude. They wished to remain as rural or semi-rural as possible and so were well content that the Bill excluded them from the conurbations. Another political complaint raised the charge of gerrymandering: it was said that the Conservative Government had designed boundaries which would give them local political advantage. This claim could have some justification in that county boroughs, normally Labour, were merged in counties normally Conservative. However, the charge lost much of its bite because Labour had also proposed to merge counties with county boroughs, although in a rather different way. In any case the political effect of a given boundary is open to dispute. It may assist one party on one side of a line and the opposing party on the other. Or it may help different parties on different occasions.

During the second reading debate in the House of Commons on the Bill the most lively issue concerned a question of procedure rather than substance: it was whether the proposals for Wales should have been presented in a separate Bill. Naturally there was much argument over matters of detail. The standing committee met on no fewer than 51 occasions. The report stage was also lengthy; many amendments were considered: the Commons sat up all night several times. But no changes of principle were made. The Government agreed to various alterations of detail. It was defeated only once in the Commons; by a majority of four an amendment was passed to give non-metropolitan districts powers in relation to refuse disposal. Later the Government successfully introduced a further amendment in the Lords to reverse this decision. So refuse disposal went to the counties. But the House of Lords were successful in forcing some changes in local boundaries. There was a flood of Government amendments, mostly minor and technical, at the end of the legislative process in the last few days of the parliamentary session. As a result some details of importance did not get a reasonable amount of consideration. Indeed, the very last stages of the Bill were notable for confusion combined with an acceptance by all parties that the Bill must be allowed to pass.

Why was this fairly general acceptance obtained? In view of the tensions caused by earlier proposals this relative harmony demands explanation. One reason, certainly, was that a general weariness had surrounded the whole question. There was broad agreement that some change was essential; that without reform local powers would be further eroded by central departments. Then the 1972 scheme was in many ways easier to accept than earlier plans. The Royal Commission had ignored the extent to which the county was a social unit as well as an administrative entity and that as a social unit it commanded considerable loyalty. In contrast the Conservative plan respected existing boundaries to a far greater extent, especially in relation to the counties. The associations of local authorities broadly accepted the plan with the exception of the Association of Municipal Corporations. And the AMC, although dissatisfied, was helpless. Amendments proposed at the committee stage designed to allocate certain county functions to former county boroughs with a minimum population of 150,000 received scant support. Of course there were many cases in which individual MPs tried to secure changes on behalf of constituency interests. Organised protest lobbies at Westminster sometimes showed a public relations flair: Herefordshire produced a Hereford bull and Plymouth paraded Drake's drum. However, with a few exceptions, these campaigns were ineffectual. They were never co-ordinated and were sometimes conflicting. Undoubtedly another factor which eased the path of the Bill was that both the Opposition and the Government backbenchers were far more concerned about other social and economic issues. In 1972 local government was far from being top of the political agenda.

So the Bill became an Act. The following chapters will outline the more important of its provisions.

Chapter III

THE BASIS OF THE SYSTEM

TYPES OF LOCAL AUTHORITY

The reformed local government system in England and Wales is based on four sub-systems which can be illustrated conveniently by diagram. The structure for the main urban centres of population is shown on the left of the page and that for the remainder of the country on the right.

Conurbations	*Mixed Urban and Rural Areas*
English Provinces	
6 Metropolitan Counties	39 Counties
|	|
36 Metropolitan Districts or Boroughs	296 Districts or Boroughs
|	|
Parishes or Towns *(in some places)*	Parishes or Towns *(except in larger urban areas)*
London	**Wales**
Greater London Council	8 Counties
|	|
32 London Boroughs	37 Districts or Boroughs
	|
	Communities or Towns *(except in larger urban areas)*

In addition to these multi-purpose authorities there exists a wide variety of special purpose bodies and joint committees formed by or in association with the major local authorities. Perhaps the most important institution of this kind is the Inner London Education Authority (ILEA) which is responsible for education in all the inner London Boroughs, i.e. those which were within the area of the former London County Council.

Changes in the structure of local government have been evolutionary rather than revolutionary. The traditional units of local administration remain—the county, the borough, the district and the parish. A map showing the top-tier boundaries of today is recognisable as a development from a map of the traditional shires. Of course there are changes. The major centres of population have produced the new metropolitan counties and in rural areas the amalgamation of counties has produced Cumbria, the new enlarged county of Cambridge and the combination Hereford and Worcester. The face of Wales, in contrast, has been changed considerably with the large-scale amalgamation of counties and the trisection of Glamorgan. The greater part of England and Wales still has a three-tier structure. This apparently cumbrous arrangement provides for a fuller range of representation of local interests and opinion than would be possible with a simpler form of organisation. It also permits functions to be distributed between the types of local authority according to the requirements of a particular service: the allocation of functions is discussed in the following section of this chapter. Areas which have but two layers of local government are those in which an urban community itself forms a second-tier authority or which has such a strong position within a second-tier authority that it is not felt to need further, separate representation. The very smallest parishes, or in Wales the smallest communities, with a population below 300 do not have a council unless a parish meeting resolves to have one. Where the population is below 200 the consent of the district council is also required. Districts exercise some general supervision over their parishes, e.g. in relation to boundary changes, elections and the compulsory acquisition of land. Where there is no parish council, the powers of the parish rest with an annual meeting which may appoint a committee to carry out any of its business.

Some districts enjoy the dignity of being boroughs. The chairmen and vice-chairmen of these councils are entitled to the status of Mayor and Deputy Mayor. To become a borough a district council must submit a petition to the Privy Council and the decision to do so must be supported by not less than two-thirds of the members voting thereon at a special meeting of the council convened for this particular purpose. If the view of the Privy Council is favourable, the district then receives a charter which may contain local provisions which appeared in earlier charters belonging to former boroughs now included within the district. In fact, every application received for borough status in 1973 and 1974 was accepted. And every metropolitan district except Sefton chose to be a borough. However, the practical effect on the powers of a district arising from borough status is negligible.

Great ingenuity has been devoted to the retention of the privileges of ancient boroughs. The 1972 Act provided three means to this end. Any parish or community council, that does not represent a grouping of parishes or communities, can resolve to choose the status of a town. This is a general right and is not restricted to former boroughs. When this course is adopted, the local council becomes a town council and the chairman of the council is entitled to be known as the town mayor. Thus former boroughs that still have their own institutions at third-tier level can retain something of their old status. It follows that an area can have two mayors, i.e. wherever a parish which opts to be a town is included in a district which has applied to become a borough. But not all former borough and urban districts were permitted to have a separate third-tier council. The Government ruled that such an authority should not have more than 20,000 population or alternatively not more than one-fifth of the population of the parent district council. These guidelines were applied with some flexibility: even so, at least 100 places were refused the right to have a parish or town council. Where a former borough is not allowed to retain a third-tier council, the method of preserving its dignities depends on whether the second-tier district authority becomes a borough. If it does, the charter rights and privileges transfer automatically to the new and larger borough. Where the district is not a borough, the district councillors elected to represent the former borough become charter trustees who are a corporate body, entitled to hold land and who can appoint one of their own number to be the town mayor.

One object which was prominent in the discussion which preceded the 1972 reform was the need to end the divorce between urban and rural areas. It was argued that a town which is a natural commercial, social and cultural centre for the surrounding hinterland should also be its administrative centre. At county level this aim has been achieved. At district level some authorities are wholly urban, some are essentially rural and some are mixed. The boundaries of many former county boroughs, now reduced to districts, were left unchanged in 1974. Extension of these towns to embrace adjacent rural areas would have created an obvious danger that the interests of rural communities would have been swamped by a dominant urban majority. So in some cases the distinction between town and country has remained at the second-tier level. Bath is a separate authority, an island wholly within another district: the same is true of Cambridge. Among third-tier authorities, the difference in status between town and parish tends to emphasise the urban/rural divide even more clearly than before the 1972 Act.

There are considerable variations in size within each category of local authority although these are far less bizarre than before the 1972 Act came into effect. Size can be measured in terms of acreage and population. Financial capacity is measured in terms of rateable value. Appendix A gives basic statistical information about the size of county and district authorities. Each metropolitan county exceeds one million population; the typical metropolitan district is nearer 250,000. Non-metropolitan counties average more than half a million people; a non-metropolitan district commonly has around 100,000 inhabitants. These figures give a general picture but there are extreme cases which depart a long way from the norms. The original intention was that the smallest non-metropolitan county should be Northumberland with a population of a quarter of a million. At a late stage in the passage of the Bill, the Government accepted that the Isle of Wight should be treated as a special case owing to its physical separation from the mainland. So the island is now the smallest county with a population a little above 100,000. Bristol is a quite different type of unusual case. It is the largest non-metropolitan district with a population of 425,000—more than twice that of many metropolitan districts which have much wider powers. In terms of acreage the largest authority is North Yorkshire. In England the average number of districts per non-metropolitan county is a little over seven. Essex, Kent and Lancashire each have fourteen districts, but Bedfordshire and Cleveland have four and the Isle of Wight only two. New Town areas are all within a single district with the one exception of the Central Lancashire new town based on Preston, Leyland and Chorley which is split between these districts.

The structure in Wales is similar to that in the non-metropolitan parts of England save that the minor local authorities are termed communities rather than parishes. Since the Anglican Church in Wales was disestablished in 1919, it is not fitting that a name associated with church organisation should be linked to a secular unit of local administration. The main difference is that Welsh authorities tend to be smaller in population. Powys scarcely exceeds 100,000 inhabitants and one of the districts within Powys, the former county of Radnorshire, serves only 18,000 people. The county of South Glamorgan is also unusual in that it has but two districts.

Local councillors are elected for a four-year term. Polling is normally on a Thursday. It is arguable whether apathy about local elections would be reduced by adopting the continental practice of voting on Sunday. The pattern of elections is not uniform. County authorities are elected as a whole in each fourth year after 1973 on the basis of single-member constituencies. In the districts the position is more complex. The rule in metropolitan districts is that a third of the councillors are elected in each year when there is not a county council election. Non-metropolitan districts are allowed a double choice. They can opt either for whole council elections, as the counties have, or they can have elections by thirds as in the metropolitan districts. Again, they can opt for single-member wards or multi-member wards or some combination of the two systems. The original arrangements were made after consultations with local opinion, i.e. with representatives of the former local authorities. So in these areas there may be an election each year or every other year. Under the former plan the election in three years out of four would be for district councillors; under the latter plan the timetable will run—county election, blank year, district election, blank year, county election and so on. After 1974 any resolution by a non-metropolitan district to change the existing arrangements needs a two-thirds majority to succeed. Parish and community councils, like the counties, are elected as a whole for a four-year term. They may be divided into wards; this is unusual in rural areas but normal in small towns.

The choices facing the non-metropolitan districts are worthy of further discussion. The borough tradition of the three-member wards and annual elections is favoured by political party organisations as giving local enthusiasts a regular focus for political activity which is felt to be helpful in maintaining interest. Accordingly this arrangement had been adopted in areas where party intervention in local elections is strong. However the system has major disadvantages. It necessitates larger electoral divisions and makes it more difficult for councillors and election candidates to become known to local residents. It increases the difficulties facing a non-party candidate attempting to organise his campaign. An annual election is more costly and causes more disturbance to the regular flow of council business. And where a council is run on strict party lines, if one party has a substantial majority it may be impossible to displace it at a single election, however badly it is beaten at the polls. An election at which the government is immune, even in the short term, is not an attractive concept. It must reduce public interest in the right to vote, as also does the greater frequency of elections. The one advantage that can be claimed for electing one-third of a council at a time is that it does provide some guarantee of continuity of membership and safeguards against the return of a very inexperienced assembly of councillors. No advantages can be claimed for the London borough system of whole council elections based on three-member wards: this could only have merit if some form of proportional representation or single alternative vote were to be introduced.

The representative responsibility of a county councillor may be more individual than that of a district councillor elected as one of three ward representatives for an urban area. The county councillor has to travel to the county capital to fulfil his duties and becomes something of an envoy to a higher authority: to a lesser extent the same is true of a parish representative on the district council. All this should mean that county elections are more keenly fought than other elections because the winners have functions which are more vital and important than those who serve on other types of local authority. In the past, county council elections have been more often unopposed than borough and urban district elections. The explanation is probably twofold: there is less party political activity in rural areas and because the county authority seems remote and distant there is less appreciation of the wide range of its activities. It still, however, remains true that the consultation of local opinion by county councillors can be a more complex activity than similar consultation in districts. Where a council is controlled by politics a councillor must pay attention to the views of his party colleagues and supporters. In rural areas, where politics are less pervasive, a county councillor will feel he should keep in touch with the attitudes of his parish councils, the district council and other local associations within his constituency. There is much overlapping of membership between the layers of local government in the counties. Some county councillors serve on district councils; many district councillors serve on parish councils.

In the historical chapter it was noted that parishes often resisted being drawn into larger authorities, partly because they resented the loss of independence but perhaps even more because it was feared that any co-operation with neighbouring parishes would prove disadvantageous financially. Today the administrative county acts as a financial pool for the county districts within its boundaries. Counties spend far more money than districts but the latter have the task of levying the local rate. The counties impose a uniform rate on the districts. In consequence the more wealthy areas of the county tend to subsidise less well-to-do places. A prosperous town will make a proportionately greater contribution to county revenue than the ratio of its population to that of the whole of the county. This situation can generate hard feelings. Every part of a county area will wish to ensure that it is enjoying its fair share of county expenditure. Equally, the claims of a county councillor to secure benefits for his area must be judged in relation to the needs of the authority as a whole. Very often the interests of the county, especially in planning matters, will diverge from more local interests. If county councillors feel a strong need to press 'constituency' questions, who is to protect the interests of the county? There are a number of possible safeguards. Where party politics are a dominant influence, the majority party, one hopes, will take a broad view. On items of expenditure the processes of financial control impose restraint. Elsewhere it may be that chief officials exercise considerable sway over the conduct of affairs and help to stifle unreasonable local claims.

Before 1972 a major difficulty facing local government was that administrative areas remained relatively static and failed to adjust to movements of population. The suburbs of an expanding town frequently spilled over its boundaries into the surrounding rural area. While this was both inconvenient and inefficient it also failed to arouse demands for appropriate adjustments to be made. Indeed, public opinion was likely to be aroused only when proposals were made to change boundaries. To work in the town and live in the adjacent rural district had a curious status value. Further, rateable values in rural areas were often lower for historical rather than practical reasons. An allied consequence of population movements in both urban and rural areas was that, as electoral divisions tended to be static, councillors came to represent very unequal numbers of electors. Ward councillors from decaying urban centres represented fewer and fewer people while those from the new suburbs were responsible to more and more. This produced undemocratic unfairness.

To deal with such matters in the future, the 1972 Act established two permanent Boundary Commissions, one for England and one for Wales. Each Commission must make regular reviews of district and county areas within every ten to fifteen years—or otherwise as the appropriate Secretary of State may direct. Local authorities and the general public must be fully consulted during the progress of these reviews and any Orders authorising boundary changes will be submitted for parliamentary approval. Alterations in parish or community areas will be suggested by the parent district council for the approval of the Boundary Commission. Should a district fail to make proposals, then the Commissions have reserve powers to act in default. Similarly the Commissions are to review regularly the electoral areas within local authorities and must be consulted about proposals from non-metropolitan districts to alter the local method of election.

One anticipates that there will be a considerable amount of work for the Boundary Commissions. Because the 1972 reorganisation of districts was carried out at high speed, many existing boundaries, although unsatisfactory, were left unchanged both in the interests of immediate administrative simplicity but also, no doubt, in order to minimise objections to the whole scheme of reform.

FUNCTIONS AND THEIR ALLOCATION

Local authority services fall into four groups which can be termed protective, communal, personal and trading. The paragraphs below describe these functions in general terms.

The first group of services is designed to protect the individual from a variety of dangers—e.g. fire, assault, robbery and epidemics. Thus local authorities provide a fire brigade, a police force, drainage, refuse removal, food inspectors and weights and measures inspectors. These protective services constitute some of the older branches of local administration, although rural areas lacked a comprehensive fire service until 1938 as before then much reliance was put on voluntary arrangements. Protective functions are negative in character as they promote good via the suppression of evil. All are highly necessary but scarcely exciting. The licensing of theatres, cinemas and of other premises for music and dancing has dual purpose. It is a safety measure and is also used to protect public morals. A local authority can prohibit the public exhibition of a film it judges to be offensive: this creates anomalies since licensing authorities do not always take the same view about the same film.

Communal services again provide benefit for all, but in a more positive way. In earlier centuries trade and travel were assisted by parish responsibility for the roads. The towns repaired and lighted the streets. Today the geographical distribution of population and employment is guided by planning authorities, the beauty of the countryside is protected and facilities are provided to assist its enjoyment. Parks and sports grounds are also provided, particularly in urban areas.

Personal services are of direct assistance to those individuals who need them. They form the most costly sector of local government functions. Education is the most expensive item. Other personal services include welfare services for children, the aged and the disabled. The use of these is optional. A parent need not send his children to a local authority school. A frail old lady living on her own need not apply for a home help. But the percentage of people who decide not to make use of public services is declining. Some services are free; others are partially subsidised. All are financed from the local rate fund supplemented by national grants. Where a charge is made, e.g. home helps, it may be wholly or partly remitted subject to a means test. Thus the personal services have an important equalising effect on society in that they benefit the poor at the expense of the rich—or the richer; they benefit the sick and the family man at the expense of the healthy and the childless; they benefit those who use public services at the expense of those who do not although entitled to do so. Over the years the development of free services has been urged forward by left-wing opinion. There is now pressure for these benefits to be provided on a selective basis so they are paid for by people who can afford it. Local authorities are tending to operate the means test principle more fully.

Trading services have declined since the nationalisation of gas and electricity in the post-war period. In 1974 water undertakings were transferred to the new Regional Water Authorities. However, in London and the metropolitan counties local authority control over passenger transport has been strengthened in recent years. Many local councils also subsidise passenger services, but this is a social welfare provision not a trading activity!

The division of local functions into these four groups is useful for the purposes of analysis, but the allocation of a particular service between the groups can be a matter of opinion. In a sense, all of them are communal. Education is provided for individuals, but it is a matter of communal benefit to have an educated society. And whether housing is regarded as a personal service or a trading undertaking must depend on how far council tenants pay an economic, i.e. unsubsidised, rent. Clearly, the sale of council houses is a trading activity. A few years ago it was arguable that town and county planning should be termed a protective service since it concentrated on stopping bad things, e.g. ribbon development; now it promotes environmental improvement and should be classed as a positive communal service. The introduction of tolls on new bridges is something of a reversion to the turnpikes and produces the flavour of a trading service.

Communal and personal services are those which show recent growth and these sectors offer wide and challenging opportunities for local government in the future.

It must also be noted that local authorities are not merely executive agencies. They exist not only to carry out duties but also to express opinions. This representative function has two forms. Local authorities can urge other public bodies to carry out policies which will be of local advantage. A Regional Planning Council can be asked to encourage industrial development in a particular area: Regional Traffic Commissioners can be asked to stop proposed fare increases on the buses. The second aspect of this representational activity is for one local authority to ask another, usually a larger authority, to do something. Counties receive many requests from districts. The executive tasks of a parish are small, but a parish council may be very active in pressing local problems on district or county councils.

Setting aside the minor authorities, the parishes and the communities in Wales, the essence of the local government system is the division of functions between two tiers of authorities, the counties and the districts. On what basis are functions distributed? The more expensive services tend to be allocated to authorities with greater financial resources. Specialised services, required by few people or which demand the use of highly skilled staff in short supply, go to authorities with substantial population. The top tier also has responsibility for functions which are felt to demand most uniformity or perhaps greater control by central government: the police are an obvious example. The second-tier authorities are responsible for services when local knowledge and responsiveness to local needs are held to be of paramount importance. Which of these criteria apply most forcibly to any particular local function must be a matter of opinion. Spokesmen for counties and districts argued these issues at length during the protracted discussions on local government reform.

The following paragraphs explain in general terms the distribution of functions under the terms of the Local Government Act, 1972. Formal lists of functions are given in Appendix B. However two preliminary points must be made. Distribution is not uniform as between upper-tier and lower-tier authorities because of statutory differences between metropolitan and non-metropolitan areas and, to a less extent, because of variations in Wales. Nor are duties uniform as between local authorities in the same sub-group because the 1972 Act gives a general power to authorities to arrange for another local authority to carry out specified duties on an agency basis. This power of transfer is subject to exceptions—the administration of education and the social services, the right to levy a rate, to raise a loan and, curiously, functions under the Diseases of Animals Act, 1850.

Non-metropolitan counties are responsible for education, libraries and social services, but not so the metropolitan counties. The financial effect is dramatic. The former account for 85 per cent of expenditure in their areas, the latter for only 20 per cent. It follows that the second-tier in the metropolitan areas is significantly more important. London follows the metropolitan pattern save that education in the inner London area is controlled by a committee of the GLC representing the inner London boroughs. Wales follows the non-metropolitan pattern. Another distinction is that metropolitan counties are passenger transport authorities: elsewhere this function is performed, if at all, by districts. However, all counties are responsible for promoting public transport policy in conjunction with bus operators and British Rail.

All counties are police and fire brigade authorities. (In London the Metropolitan Police are the direct responsibility of the Home Secretary.) Consumer protection, including the inspection of weights and measures, food and drugs, is another general field of county activity except in London and sometimes in Wales. Minor items on the list are road safety and the provision of small holdings. Some counties have special duties in connection with National Parks.

Other functions are shared between counties and districts, notably planning and highways. Counties prepare structure plans which determine the broad strategy of development for their areas: districts prepare local plans which set out more precisely the detailed implementation of county policy. Districts also decide whether to grant development permission, except where an application is of sufficient importance to raise issues which affect county policy, in which case the matter is transmitted for decision by the county planning authority. Districts issue enforcement orders and revocations of planning permission. Both counties and districts have powers in relation to town development. Another example of shared responsibility relates to abandoned motor vehicles; districts remove them but counties destroy them. This is a particular application of the general principle that districts collect refuse but counties destroy it. Counties are the major highway authorities and are responsible for road maintenance. Districts can claim to maintain unclassified roads in urban areas, i.e. the territory of former boroughs and urban districts: this work is carried out at county expense but subject to county cost control. Counties are responsible for local traffic orders and control of parking but districts have concurrent powers, with county consent, to provide off-street car parks. Other concurrent powers relate to recreation and leisure facilities, swimming baths, open spaces and entertainments, aerodromes and action in natural emergencies.

District functions also cover environmental and public health services, including building regulations, clean air, drainage and inspection of offices, shops and factories. Housing is perhaps the most important duty. Counties, except in Wales, have reserve housing powers but these can be used only on the request of a district council. Districts collect the rate. They can operate buses where local powers existed before 1972; in addition they can subsidise services and provide travel concessions. They can provide allotments, markets and civic restaurants, and are responsible for coast protection.

Districts are licensing authorities for theatres, cinemas, night refreshment houses and many other purposes. Welsh districts have an additional significance for they constitute the areas for holding septennial referenda to determine whether alcohol should be on public sale on Sunday in licensed premises.

Individual local authorities may obtain additional powers through private Bill legislation: this procedure is described in the following chapter. Otherwise local government is bound by a firm *ultra vires* rule which forbids the spending of money other than in ways authorised by statute. Even so there is some flexibility in that a county or district can spend up to the amount realised by the rate of 2p on any purpose which is in the interests of its area. Expenditure under this heading may include contributions to charity.

Overall the 1972 Act marked a further stage in the process of making local government less local. It reduced the number of top-tier county level authorities to less than 40 per cent of the previous total. As metropolitan districts retain education and social services, the cut in the number of authorities responsible for these functions was not quite so severe. However, the statutory provisions which permitted and sometimes required delegation of county powers have also been withdrawn. Powers over traffic orders were also moved from districts to counties. In sum, the total of centralisation was considerable. Even more serious from the local government standpoint was the loss of further functions from the ambit of local government, namely personal health services, water supply and sewerage.

To be fair, the 1972 Act did provide for some decentralisation. Previously many districts had exercised some delegated powers in relation to town and country planning but the Act gave them control over planning questions that do not affect county policy. In view of the growing public interest in planning matters, this is a major advance for district councils. Some licensing duties have also been handed down from counties to districts, and, as noted above, there is the possibility of agency arrangements to carry out county duties.

To conclude with, a review of the activities of the minor local authorities, the parishes and communities. Their powers are optional and of limited importance. They include provision and maintenance of allotments, burial grounds, public clocks, footpaths, bus shelters, recreation grounds, street lighting and war memorials. In addition they have various powers in relation to charities and common or parish land. But a major part of the business of the minor authorities is to represent local opinion to other local authorities and public bodies. It follows that parish and community councils can and do discuss many items which fall outside the scope of their executive duties. In particular they can claim to be consulted on local planning applications. There is no doubt that a vigorous parish or community council can play a valuable role in protecting the rural environment and it provides an opportunity to ventilate opinion which is sadly lacking in the wards of our large boroughs.

COUNTY/DISTRICT RELATIONSHIPS

The harmony of a two-tier local government structure is greatly influenced by the quality of co-operation between county and district councils. Both represent local opinion, albeit over different areas. Both share functions, especially planning, which cannot be exercised independently of each other. They can achieve important economies if they agree to share specialised resources. Yet there are serious hindrances to co-operation, namely separate institutional loyalties, sometimes party political differences and a widespread instinct amongst the district councils to preserve and insist upon their independence.

Closer relationships between the two tiers can be assisted through a variety of methods. There is some common membership between the two types of authorities as some councillors have been elected to both district and county councils. One local authority can provide goods and services for another; this provision facilitates joint purchasing arrangements, the joint use of computers and the employment of both district and county staff upon a particular project. Section 101 of the Local Government Act 1972 allowed one local authority to act as the agent of another local authority in the provision of services: the difficulties of this arrangement are considered below. Finally, two or more local authorities can appoint a joint committee to help them to find a common approach to particular problems.

Many counties have formed such joint committees with their districts to discuss items of mutual interest. These committees may cover a whole county or be restricted to a single district. They may constitute a general forum of discussion on local government affairs or they can be restricted to a particular function. They are purely advisory and have no executive functions. It may therefore be difficult to find useful work for them to do. They can too readily be used simply to complain about what other people are doing or not doing. There are also problems of organisation. If a single committee is used to cover a whole county and the county has equal representation with each district, then the county will be heavily outnumbered. If county representation equals that of all the districts together, then the burden of attendance on county councillors will be severe. Again, if a county establishes a separate committee for each district then the cost is heavy in terms of the time of both county councillors and county officials. Necessarily this problem is aggravated in the counties with a large number of districts, e.g. Essex, Hampshire and Kent. Where the remit of a committee is very broad, there is also a problem over the continuity of membership. Where membership is static a committee may not contain local representatives whose experience and interests are most appropriate for the business of a particular meeting: if membership is fluid and can be adjusted to suit the agenda, the committee tends to lose continuity and become a series of *ad hoc* gatherings.

Some counties have decentralised the administration of a particular service, e.g. highways. Such an arrangement may be accompanied by the establishment of area committees with responsibility for supervising the local operation of the county service. Where this is done the district councils may be invited to nominate a few members of the area committees, and so are given a modest opportunity to influence county policy. The joint committees described in the previous paragraph should be carefully distinguished from the area committees. The former are purely advisory bodies; the latter are county sub-committees with some executive responsibility.

The problems caused by concurrent powers continue to give trouble. Such powers provide splendid opportunities for co-operation between counties and districts; equally they can provide a climate in which mutual inaction flourishes. The danger of inertia arises from the possibility that a council may lose enthusiasm for a service in the hope that the other tier will exert itself and carry the financial burden. The list of these concurrent functions includes museums, art galleries, the acquisition of land, clearance of derelict sites, health education, aerodromes, action in face of natural emergencies and provision for recreation. The catalogue does not include major local government services but in total it amounts to a significant opportunity to improve the quality of life. One method of avoiding friction over these shared responsibilities is for the two tiers to strike a bargain. Thus in Tyne and Wear the arrangement is that the county shall be responsible for museums and art galleries while the districts provide leisure facilities which cater for physical exertion unless a district asks the county to take over a major project which will serve needs from outside the district.

It was noted above that planning powers are shared between counties and districts: counties are responsible for the formulation of broad strategy and districts deal with the detailed application of county policy. To examine in detail the problems of a particular local service would be to go beyond the scope of this book. But it must be stressed that this partnership in planning requires full co-operation between the two tiers if it is to work well. Counties want to be satisfied that decisions by districts do not undermine county policy; they may well be unhappy about development permission given or withheld on particular sites. Equally, district councillors and planning staff may be better informed about the local environment and local opinion than are the county personnel: certainly they may feel better qualified to take local planning decisions. The employment of separate teams of planning officials who spend much time negotiating with each other is clearly wasteful. So the Conservative Government elected in 1979 decided to redefine the distribution of planning powers. The ability of the counties to intervene on individual planning applications was to be greatly reduced. Districts have become the effective local planning authorities although they are guided by the broad outlines of county strategy.

THE COMMITTEE SYSTEM

Even in the smallest local authorities—other than parishes—it is obvious that all the detailed consideration of business cannot be done at meetings of the full council. Accordingly, committees are established. The tendency is for them to grow in number and in authority. They consume a great amount of time of both elected members and officers. It is commonly said that the committee is the workshop of local government: certainly, a realistic appraisal of committee behaviour is essential to a full understanding of the practice of local administration.

In the interests of speed in decision-making, the 1972 Act increased the powers that can be given to committees and to officers. A local authority may delegate its powers to a committee, sub-committee or an officer. Further, unless the authority otherwise directs, a committee may arrange for its powers to be discharged by a sub-committee or an officer: thus the principal *delegatus non potest delegare* is avoided. However, the full council cannot remit its power to levy a rate or raise a loan. In accordance with the Maud and Bains Reports (discussed in Chapter VII) the tendency now is for simplified structures with fewer committees and sub-committees and wider delegation. It is common practice to nominate a central committee, usually entitled Policy and Resources, to deal with major issues concerning the allocation of funds and to exercise a co-ordinating role of the work of the authority as a whole. The number of committees varies from council to council. Second-tier authorities in the shires tend to have fewer as they have fewer responsibilities. It is no longer usual to appoint a separate committee for each major function or local authority department. Instead the work of an authority is divided into broad 'programme areas' and a committee is allocated to each. The question then arises—can the ambit of a committee be too broad? This issue has arisen particularly with planning and transportation which some authorities have treated as one programme area to be controlled by a single committee; other authorities have felt the scope was too great for a single body and appointed separate committees.

The frequency of committee meetings also varies. They tend to be more often in the districts than in the shire counties. But every councillor knows that the routine timetable of meetings can be supplemented by others called for a special purpose. A committee once born becomes unwilling to die. It may be justifiable to have a separate body to consider a fresh and unexplored problem but when the new category of business contracts or becomes routine, the justification disappears.

Each local authority decides on the size of its committees. The larger the body, the wider the range of opinion and experience that can be represented on it. Conversely, the larger the body the smaller must be the scope for the average member to play a significant part in its work and the greater will be the cost in terms of time demanded of the elected members. Authorities in rural areas tend to have larger committees because there is pressure for the constituent geographical parts to be represented. Where a council is run on party lines the majority group will ensure that it has a political majority on each committee. Otherwise the selection of committee members should take into account their regularity of attendance and reputation with fellow council members. The central policy committee is the key committee of a council and the most senior and able members are usually selected to serve on it.

Is it useful for local authorities to inject more outside blood into their proceedings? The law permits this to be done. A council may include on its committees, other than a finance committee, persons with full voting rights who are not members of the parent council, providing that such additional members do not form more than one-third of any committee. This practice of co-option from outside does enable local authorities to widen the range of specialised knowledge and experience available for their deliberations. Magistrates form one-third of every Police Authority but this is tantamount to the creation of a joint committee rather than co-option. Otherwise the practice is optional. It is commonly used on education committees and boards of school governors and managers. (There is a widespread misconception that co-opted members are mandatory for education committees.) But apart from education, this device is not much used. One reason is a feeling that it is undemocratic to give authority to persons who have not been popularly elected. Council members may think that they can get adequate specialised advice from their officers. They may also fear that co-opted members would outshine them in discussion and have an unduly dominant role in committee decisions. Critics have also said that the system can be abused—that where councils are run on political lines, co-option can be a method of compensation for defeated council candidates. One local incident is worth recalling. In 1972 the co-opted members of the Exeter Education Committee voted with the minority Labour and Liberal groups to elect another co-opted member, said to be a left-winger, as chairman of the committee. The Conservative majority on the City Council, acting under the terms of the 1944 Education Act, thereupon successfully applied to the Secretary of State for permission to dissolve and reconstitute their Education Committee. This was done to avoid a situation in which the education chairman would not have been a member of the City Council and, indeed, would have been hostile to its political majority group. This was an exceptional occurrence. In general, the practice of bringing additional people into local committee work is valuable and should perhaps be used more widely.

Meetings of committees are held in an informal atmosphere. The chief officer responsible for the committee's business or a committee clerk will sit next to the chairman in a strategic position to offer *sotto voce* words of advice. If the body is small enough it will sit round a table. Smoking is permitted unless health warnings have had effect. At the first meeting in the council year the initial task is to elect a chairman. Where an authority is subject to political control the chairmen are chosen by the majority group—otherwise the choice depends on the interplay of personalities. The normal practice is to start proceedings by approving the minutes of the previous meeting. The other items on the agenda will be to consider developments in matters that have been previously before the committee, and new pieces of business. Information on these will either have been circulated beforehand in reports prepared by the officers or there will be a verbal report at the meeting. Sub-committee reports are usually introduced by the chairmen of sub-committees. The volume of papers circulated to members to prepare them for the business varies considerably; often it is very substantial. The Maud Committee on *Management of Local Government* reported in 1967 that one of the largest county boroughs sent out 700 sheets of paper a month to each member of the council and 1,000 sheets to those on the education committee. One wonders what proportion of the papers were read. Strenuous efforts have since been made to cut down the amount of detailed business submitted to committees, and to reduce the bulk of paper circulated. In the case of education, the status of the committee is protected by law: a local education authority is required by statute to refer all matters to its education committee and must consider the committee's recommendations before taking action, except in an emergency. So the content of committee work is mixed. It is desirable that they should concentrate on issues of major policy but much time can still be consumed on trivial items that become contentious, perhaps for political reasons.

Thus committees are separate but interrelated cogs in the local government machine. How can they be made to mesh smoothly together? This raises the allied problems of co-ordination and control. Such supervision is essential otherwise committees would become wholly independent entities. Control is vital to ensure that a council remains in full charge of its policies and expenditure. Co-ordination is needed to prevent waste. It need not involve saying 'No' to a committee, but is rather a matter of showing them that their proposals can be carried out more effectively or economically if they are done in a certain way. A problem facing one committee may already have been dealt with satisfactorily by another. One committee may find that a certain piece of land or property is surplus to requirements while another committee may be seeking to buy a similar property. At this level co-ordination is increasingly the task of chief officers although formal responsibility may rest with some form of central policy committee. At lower levels, e.g. the need to maintain steady work flows for office and outdoor staff, the responsibility must rest wholly on officials.

Control of committee policy raises other issues. All spending is subject to review by auditors, internal and external, who provide a rigorous check against irregularity. The formal process of policy control takes place at council meetings at which reports or minutes of committees are presented for approval. Where a committee has delegated powers it will present a report of its actions for the information of council members and not for approval. Practice varies as to how detailed these reports are. For obvious reasons in the larger authorities the scale of delegation is greater and less detail can be included in reports if they are not to be unduly lengthy. At the full council meeting should members object to the way in which delegated powers have been exercised they can do nothing where the delegation is absolute. Of course, the council can always withdraw the delegation.

On matters that are not delegated the council can reject a committee's proposals or refer them back for further consideration. This occurs infrequently. Time at council meetings is not limited in any strict or formal sense, but the patience and energy of elected members are limited. Were a large number of recommendations to be challenged, then meetings would become unduly long. Even so, there will be many occasions when the specialised enthusiasms of a committee will be overruled on matters of principle, on issues that affect the business of other committees and especially on levels of expenditure. How is this done? Wherever a council is run on party lines, policy supervision can be expected to come from the dominant political group which will settle its internal disputes, if necessary, by vote at its 'caucus' meetings. In the absence of strong party loyalties, the situation becomes more flexible. The general policy committee can normally persuade a council to prune back any proposals for expenditure it considers excessive. The ultimate check to a committee is imposed by the balance of opinion expressed in council debate. The council must always prevail in any fundamental clash with a committee because it holds the ultimate sanction of being able to replace recalcitrant committee members with others who will heed the views of the full council.

The committee system offers substantial advantages. It ensures that all business has been subjected to prior consideration before it comes to a council meeting and thus avoids hasty decisions. This process of pre-digestion should enable a council to devote its attention to matters of major importance. Council members can specialise on particular aspects of the authority's work, thus helping them to make a valuable contribution to it. The specialisation also leads to a deeper sense of involvement and commitment; it heightens the sense of responsibility for the committee's work. And by narrowing the ambit of concentration for the elected member, the committee system enhances his education in administration. The informal atmosphere softens differentials in status and partisan opinions. So officers can intervene in discussion and offer advice to an extent that would be resented and thought improper at council meetings. And where a local authority is dominated by party loyalty, in the freedom of committee the members will not always talk and act in party groupings.

Since a council cannot take all decisions one obvious alternative is to transfer much decision-making power to an individual, be he official or elected member. But the wisdom of any one man (or woman) acting alone is open to doubt, quite apart from the force of the dictum that power corrupts. The committee enables power to be shared and brings together a variety of interests and experience which, in most cases, should produce a better and more acceptable decision. Not all members will play an equal part in moulding the collective mind of the meeting: there will be always a few who give a lead, either through stronger personality or greater experience and ability. An adviser to the committee, a chief officer, may often persuade it. In these circumstances a committee decision is perhaps not a genuine collective decision, but is rather a 'front' or support for those people who dominate its deliberations. Yet a committee, unless completely inert, is a valuable check. The leading voices still have to convince. Without committees, far more decisions would be made without potential challenge.

Equally committees are open to criticism. There must be a tendency for each one to live in a world of its own, deeply conscious of its special problems but failing to see them in the context of the full responsibilities of the council. They may be swayed too easily by the advice of officials, backed by the authority of professional qualifications which can produce undue enthusiasm and ill-balanced judgement. There is always a danger that a committee may seek to build an empire and be over-concerned with matters of status. The safeguards are to establish a central policy or executive committee to oversee other committees and to have as few committees and departments as possible. Thus the Seebohm Report of 1968 recommended that all social services provided by local government be administered through a single committee: this idea became a requirement in the Local Authority Social Services Act, 1970.

It was noted above that the power to delegate decisions to the committees is widely used. But how far should committees themselves deal with the detailed application of general policy, or how far should these matters be left to officials? The extent to which officials are permitted to act will vary. In larger authorities, delegation to officials has increased both in order to save time and to prevent committees being overburdened with detail. But there is some unwillingness among elected representatives to surrender prerogatives. There is a widespread conception of local democracy, dating from the Victorian era, which insists that it is the duty of elected representatives to take all decisions; that it is undemocratic to allow officials to exercise discretion. And some councillors do not wish to surrender matters to officials because they like dealing with details and personal cases.

A substantial cost has to be paid for any insistence that elected representatives must take decisions. Committee meetings are longer; sub-committees multiply; mounds of paper are distributed to explain the detailed business to committee members; officials spend much time in preparing these papers; if they are conscientious, committee members must spend much time on studying agendas and reports; decisions are delayed until committees, and sometimes the full council, have met. All this might be tolerable were it certain that decisions would be made under optimum conditions. Unhappily this is not the case. Often elected representatives may be less qualified to take decisions than the officers who advise them. This statement has an undemocratic flavour but frequently it must be true. Normally a happy marriage between democratic principle and expertise is possible since committees accept the advice of their professional staff. A committee would not dispute the view of its surveyor that a bridge was unsafe. School governors and managers commonly think it improper to intervene on questions of curriculum. Yet this self-denying convention may break down. What is the best course of action to take in relation to a child in care? Here any committee member may feel that his opinion is as valuable as that of an official. When a committee is faced with an aesthetic issue it is a matter of opinion whether professional advice should necessarily be followed. There is great variety in the extent to which elected members concern themselves with staff appointments, including teachers: it is arguable that this is a type of responsibility that chief officials should be expected to shoulder. There is a danger that when committee members become involved in personal cases emotion may determine action, or an undesirable element of patronage or even corruption may creep into council business. Housing is an obvious example. If council tenancies are decided by officials operating a points scheme, no favouritism is likely to arise; if a housing committee or subcommittee arranges tenancies, the basis of decisions becomes a matter for speculation.

Over-devotion to detail gives elected representatives inadequate time to concentrate on major matters of policy. Committee members snowed under with papers containing information on trivial matters will have less time to read more important documents, e.g. Ministry circulars. Indeed, where circulars are not immediately relevant to committee business, members may never know of the existence of a circular or will not appreciate its contents. Likewise at meetings, if hours are consumed by the minor items on the agenda, inadequate time is left for important business. A wily official may put a difficult matter of policy at the end of an agenda in the hope that he can persuade a tired committee to follow a certain line of action. Some committees, the weak committees, may prefer to take time over fairly routine items and then get through the major business rapidly by following the advice of their staff because the major items are too complex for members to be able to debate effectively.

In theory, one can argue that committees should decide policy and leave their officials to carry out the details of administration. In practice, the distinction between policy and administration can never be clear-cut. At what stage does a decision on how to put a policy into practice become itself a policy decision? If unexpected administrative difficulties develop which involve additional expenditure, the elected representatives must be consulted. If the operation of a policy incurs unexpected difficulties with the public, the councillors will need to know.

Under the reformed local government system the local authorities are fewer in number and larger in size, so councillors must place increasing trust on the judgement of their officers. This principle is now widely admitted, even where the need for it is regretted. But not all the problems raised in this chapter can be solved by leaving

matters to officials. The influence of the Bains Report on the relationships between committees and chief officers is discussed in Chapter
VII.

THE ASSOCIATIONS OF LOCAL AUTHORITIES

Towards the end of the nineteenth century each category of local
authorities formed an association for mutual support and assistance. The 1972 reorganisation also provided a unique opportunity
to reform these associations. One possibility was that they might
join into a single body, perhaps with a federal constitution. The
advantages of such a move were apparent. There would be a
great simplification in the structure of the joint organisations
which the associations had formed or on which they were represented. The development of further nationally-based services to
local councils would be facilitated. There would be administrative economies. Above all, local government would be able to
speak to central government and the general public with a single
and far more powerful voice. Discussions were held between the
associations to see if a basis of unity could be found. However,
no agreement was reached largely for political reasons. All the
metropolitan counties and most of the metropolitan districts
returned Labour majorities at the 1973 elections. So the leaders
of these councils came to favour a separate national organisation
for metropolitan areas in the knowledge that such a body would
normally be dominated by the Labour Party. The Greater
London Council, which previously had stood apart from the
associations, agreed to join. So also did the London boroughs.
Thus the Association of Metropolitan Authorities was born.
When it became clear that unity among all types of authorities
was impossible, the shire counties formed the Association of
County Councils and likewise the districts formed the Association of District Councils. The third-tier authorities are now represented through the National Association of Local Councils which
serves parish councils, town councils and community councils in
Wales.

These associations have a wide variety of functions. They
provide advice for individual local authorities. They give an
opportunity to exchange opinions and experience about current
problems. They provide representation on the wide range of
public bodies and advisory committees that are in some way
connected with local government. They co-operate with each
other and so provide a united policy for some aspects of local
administration. The associations nominate representatives on the

myriad of National Joint Councils which bargain over salaries, wages and conditions of employment for all those on the payroll of local authorities.

The main task of the associations is to negotiate with each other and with government departments about proposals to change the law or any administrative practices concerning local government. In particular they engage in detailed negotiations with civil servants over the amount of financial assistance local government is to receive from the Exchequer through the rate support grant. Each association is in touch with a number of MPs who may be asked, on appropriate occasions, to put forward in the House of Commons the point of view of a particular category of local authority. It is easy to overlook these activities and to underrate their significance, because much of the work is done in private and does not receive great publicity. In fact, central departments do not generally introduce a change in policy—unless it be a major political decision—without some prior and semi-confidential discussions with the associations. Should the latter be firmly united in opposition to government proposals, then Ministers often make adjustments so that their policy becomes more acceptable. While the associations are often in conflict with government departments, every effort is made to keep relationships as harmonious as possible. They try to evade issues which are not strictly local government matters and they also avoid becoming entangled in a dispute between any one local authority and a Ministry unless there are general principles involved of general concern.

The associations have formed a number of joint bodies each with a specialised purpose and known by a code name devised from the initial letters in the formal title of the organisation. A glossary may be useful:

CCLEA   Central Council of Local Education Authorities
CCLGF   Central Council on Local Government Finance
JACLAP   Joint Advisory Committee for Local Authorities Purchasing
LACSAB   Local Authorities Conditions of Service Advisory Board
LAMIT   Local Authorities Mutual Investment Trust
LAMSAC   Local Authorities Management Services Advisory Committee
LGTB   Local Government Training Board.

The first two of these bodies require particular attention. The first enables all education authorities to meet together, discuss common problems, evolve common policies and press agreed positions on Ministers and other bodies connected with educational development. No other local authority service has a separate organisation of this importance. CCLEA was established in 1974 when it effectively took over the functions of the Association of Education Committees; the AEC was formed in 1902 at the time of the Balfour Education Act and over the years had been a highly influential body. CCLGF, created in 1975, differs from all the other bodies noted here because of the extent of participation by the central government. The chairman is the Secretary of State for the Environment. He is supported by other Ministers and officials from this department and all the other government departments concerned with local government. It is this body which undertakes the complex negotiations about levels of local expenditure and the size and distribution of the rate support grant. There is some element of secrecy surrounding its business. Ministers and civil servants hope that an air of confidentiality will reduce the party political element in discussions: local authority representatives hope that a cloak of confidence may make their representations more effective because central government are more likely to concede points in private than in public. Without doubt the CCLGF, together with its various subgroups, provides the major forum for the interchange of views between central and local authorities. It symbolises the tendency to centralise local affairs.

As local authorities have become more dominated by party political loyalties, so also have the associations of local authorities. Their political balance will change with the swing of the political pendulum. The AMA is more likely to be controlled by the Labour Party than are the ACC or the ADC. It is very helpful to Ministers if their own party is in command of the major local authority associations.

Chapter IV

CENTRAL CONTROL OF LOCAL GOVERNMENT

To a large extent our system of local government has been a system of local *self* government. There is a strong tradition that local communities should be able to decide how to deal with their own problems. In the introductory historical chapter it was shown how the central guiding hand of Chadwick was deeply resented. Today central supervision has come to be accepted in general terms although complaints are still frequent about particular applications of it. Clearly, if the national government did not have ultimate control over local councils the latter would tend to become autonomous units. No sovereign state would tolerate such a basic challenge to its authority unless it was prepared to become a federation of largely independent communities. At the other extreme, if local government were to have no ambit of decision not dominated by national government—then it would cease to be local *government* at all and become a mere agent of national government. So central-local relations demand a balance of control and independence, a balance of partnership and separation. The examination of why these relationships have evolved towards their present pattern is left until the final chapter. The immediate purpose is to describe the network of controls that surround local authorities.

One other preliminary note is essential. The orthodox treatment of central control divided it into three sectors, control by Parliament, Government Departments and the Courts. This fits the traditional tripartite division of political institutions into the legislature, the executive and the judiciary. However, if this model induces the idea that local government has three sets of controllers—Members of Parliament, civil servants and judges—then it is misleading. Civil servants advise Ministers how to use the powers made available to them by Act of Parliament. Members of Parliament are heavily influenced by party loyalty, so that the Commons normally accept the policy proposed by Ministers of the Government. Not all legislation is initiated by Ministers and the formal process of party discipline, the use of the whips, is not applied to Bills sponsored by backbenchers or by local authorities. But no Bill in either of these categories will pass if Ministers are deeply hostile to it. Thus both parliamentary and administrative controls over local government reflect the will of Ministers. Judicial control is a separate category; yet here again if Ministers dislike a judicial interpretation of local government law they could use their parliamentary majority to amend the law.

The threefold distinction between parliamentary, administrative and judicial control is retained in the pages that follow as it facilitates description. But it must not be forgotten that while civil servants, Members of Parliament and judges are not without influence, the essence of national supervision of local government is that it is undertaken on behalf of the Ministers of Her Majesty's Government.

PARLIAMENTARY CONTROL

The legal basis of national control over local government is that local authorities have no powers other than those conferred on them by statute. All local councils must be able to produce statutory authority for everything they do. If a council exceeds its powers, albeit unwittingly, its actions may be challenged in court where the principle of *ultra vires* will be invoked, and the extra-legal actions will be declared null and void. Thus local authorities largely carry out the administration of general principles of policy decided by the national legislature. Local authorities are not themselves legislative— i.e. rule-making—bodies except in relation to local bye-laws, and even here their decisions are subject to detailed government scrutiny and approval.

Local government law is complex, partly because it is highly detailed, partly because there are many varieties in the forms of legal power. Some statutory authority is contained in the Acts which established a particular type of local council. Thus the Greater London Council and the London Boroughs received powers from the London Government Act, 1963. More generally, however, powers are obtained from general Acts relating to a specific local authority function; obvious examples are the major statutes relating to public health, education and town and country planning. Most of the duties conferred on local authorities by Parliament are mandatory, i.e. compulsory, but in a few matters of secondary importance there is a choice of whether to use or 'adopt' powers. The Small Dwellings Acquisition Act, 1899, which enabled councils to provide mortgage loans to encourage home ownership, is an example of this optional arrangement. Another more recent case is the ability of the rating authorities to decide under the terms of the Local Government Act, 1966, whether to levy rates on unoccupied properties. In 1963 Parliament gave local authorities a general optional power to spend a penny rate in any way for the benefit of its area provided that such activity was not subject to other statutory limitations: the 1972 Act increased the permitted rate to two new pence. A third type of power is that conferred by a local Act, where Parliament has accepted a request by a local authority to give it additional authority. The procedure for obtaining such special powers is complicated and expensive; generally speaking, only the larger authorities seek to promote their own private Bills. A few pioneering ventures, notably the Birmingham Municipal Bank, have been started in this way, but many of the powers obtained from private Bills are relatively minor and raise no points of principle. The intention behind Section 262 of the Local Government Act 1972 was to enforce drastic simplification in this area. The plan is for a Government Bill to confer generally on local authorities those local Act powers which are found to be of value. Meanwhile local councils are due to consider which of their remaining local powers need to be retained. The residue of unnecessary and outdated local legislation will then be repealed—in metropolitan areas by 1979 and in the shires by 1984.

Private Bill procedure, if widely used, could have greatly broadened the span of local government. Perhaps this is why Parliament has ensured that the promotion of a private Bill is a formidable obstacle race. A resolution to promote a Bill must be passed at two council meetings by a majority of the members and public notices must be issued indicating the nature of the powers a council hopes to acquire. If all these hurdles are surmounted, a private Bill goes before Parliament where, having been scrutinised by a body of Examiners to see it is in appropriate form, it then has to go through the usual routine of three readings in both Houses. Normally these readings are a formality. Discussion is usually restricted to the committee stage which is held before a small group of Members who sit in a quasijudicial capacity hearing arguments in support of the Bill and any objections to it. Pleadings for and against a Bill are undertaken by members of the 'parliamentary bar', a special kind of barrister. The need to employ these parliamentary counsel adds greatly to the cost of the proceedings, especially if a Bill arouses objections and the committee stage is protracted. It was shown above that a Bill will not succeed if it incurs ministerial hostility; however, ministerial support is not an absolute guarantee of success, especially as the Bill has to satisfy the Lords as well as the Commons. The Conservative interest in Parliament has tended to be hostile to new extensions of local authority activity, notably in relation to municipal trading.

In addition to powers obtained directly from statutes, local government receives further powers from various types of Orders made by Ministers—Provisional Orders, Orders under the Statutory Orders

(Special Procedure) Act, 1945, and normal Statutory Instruments. These are subject to varying degrees of parliamentary scrutiny. However, since they all engage the influence of Ministers, it is unusual for any parliamentary challenge to be successful. Many Orders of purely local application, e.g. compulsory purchase and clearance orders, asked for by local authorities, are approved or not approved by Ministers, and are not submitted to Parliament at all.

ADMINISTRATIVE CONTROLS

The detailed supervision of the work of local authorities is undertaken by government departments. The extent of the direction varies greatly from function to function and between different parts of the same function. Central government is deeply involved in all major issues relating to education, police and town and country planning; it pays far less attention to the provision of public libraries, municipal entertainments and recreational facilities. The Department of the Environment is concerned with the amount of local authority housebuilding and the standards of design and construction, but local authorities are wholly free to select tenants on whatever basis they think best. It is also greatly concerned with major road improvements (trunk roads are entirely a government responsibility) but leaves alone the maintenance of minor roads. This variation is due largely to the uneven amount of political interest attracted by local government functions and, inevitably, the more expensive services will induce greatest attention.

Most of the supervisory activity by the central government is authorised specifically by statute, but there are a few examples of Ministers being entrusted by Parliament with a broad oversight of a particular local government function. The Local Authority Social Services Act, 1970, is the most authoritarian piece of local government law to have been passed in recent years. It requires the responsible authorities to appoint a social services committee, restricts the business coming before the committee subject to the consent of the Secretary of State, empowers the Secretary of State to prescribe qualifications to be held by a director of social services and requires local authorities to act under general ministerial guidance in relation to these functions. The Education Act, 1944, is another extreme example of conferring wide power on a Minister by generalised wording. According to the Act it is the duty of the Secretary of State for Education 'to secure the effective execution by local authorities, under his control and direction, of the national policy for providing a varied and comprehensive educational service in every area'. (In view of the current controversy about comprehensive education, it must be stressed that the word 'comprehensive' in the Education Act was used in the normal sense of all-embracing, not in the recent specialised sense which implies the abolition of selection for secondary education.) The language of the Act is strong and scarcely fits the conception that local authorities should govern: rather it implies that local education authorities are mere agents to carry out a Minister's will. This impression is supported by another section of the Act which authorises the Secretary of State if satisfied that any local education authority '. . . have acted or are proposing to act unreasonably' to give directions accordingly. In fact, these draconian powers are not used. Yet they remain in the background and must overshadow any major dispute between the Department and local education authorities.

The Education Act, 1944, is vague in another important sense. It speaks of the national policy for education without defining what the policy is to be. Presumably the policy is to be decided, and redefined from time to time, by the responsible Minister. Thus the wide powers of the 1944 Act entitle the Secretary of State for Education and Science to press forward or restrain the ending of selection for secondary education depending on the viewpoint of the Government.

Many other Acts give Ministers a strong reserve power over local authorities. If a Minister is satisfied that a council has failed to perform a particular function adequately he may be empowered to issue an order to the council to instruct it to do certain things, or he may transfer powers from a district council to a county council or he may take over the powers himself. This default power was first incorporated in the Public Health Act, 1875, in respect of sewerage and water supply but was never actually used. Similar provisions are to be found *inter alia* in the Public Health Act, 1936, the Town and Country Planning Acts, 1947 and 1962, the Civil Defence Act, 1948, and the Housing Finance Act, 1972. These certainly give Ministers a big stick to brandish at recalcitrant local councils, but they are called into effect very rarely; post-war examples relate to civil defence at Coventry and St Pancras and, more recently, to housing at Clay Cross. There is no difference between the political parties in the matter of these broad statutory powers over local government: both Conservative and Labour Governments have inserted default clauses into local government legislation.

In the nineteen-forties it was the fashion for major Acts dealing with local government functions to require local authorities to prepare development plans for ministerial approval. The idea was to force councils to take a long-term look at local conditions and to get them to commit themselves in advance to a programme of improvement. The practical effect of these development schemes varied considerably. The plans for future school-building rapidly became out-of-date and were ignored. Long-term plans drawn up under the Town and Country Planning Acts, although repeatedly changed, are the basis of all town and country planning controls. More recently in 1972 the DHSS asked local authorities responsible for the provision of social services to prepare ten-year plans which would chart the course of future growth of these services; the Department also suggested standards of provision which local authorities should attempt to achieve.

One of the oldest forms of central supervision is the use of inspection, first employed by Chadwick in 1834 to review the activities of the Boards of Guardians. Four local authority services are subject to regular inspection, police, fire, education, children. There are two aspects to an inspector's duties. Primarily he has to ensure that local services are efficient and that standards are maintained: he also advises local authorities and his own Department on matters of technique and policy improvement. The term 'inspector' is also used, rather misleadingly, to describe officials who preside over local enquiries of various kinds. Their task is essentially to hear objections to proposals and report thereon to a Minister—this function will be considered below in the paragraphs on the appellate functions of Ministers.

The process of inspection is concerned not so much with council policy as with the way in which council servants perform their duties. There are other types of control over officials. In some cases regulations prescribe their qualifications and duties. Various controls over the appointment and dismissal of local government officers are outlined below in the section describing the role of officials. The most exhaustive control over personnel is to be found in the police and fire services where the Home Secretary can make regulations governing appointment, dismissal, discipline, and conditions of service. In the case of fire brigades the supervision extends to methods of training and the provision of certain items of equipment.

Various actions of local authorities require ministerial approval. Development plans provide one example; another is any proposal for the compulsory purchase of land or property. Many Acts require a Minister to adjudicate in a conflict between a local authority and an individual, but some such disputes go to a court of law. Parliament has been careful to protect private rights against unjustifiable interference by local government, but no clear line can be drawn between the sort of issue that goes to a Minister and that which goes to a court. The policy imposed by Parliament has varied. Before 1930 appeals against closing orders—that a house is unfit for human habitation— were decided by the Ministry of Health: now they go before a county court judge. It is still a matter of doubt whether a county court judge is best suited to consider the technical issues that may arise in such disputes. A better solution might be to create a special tribunal to deal with these cases.

If an authority makes a clearance order to compulsorily acquire an area of sub-standard housing and other property for the purpose of redevelopment, any appeal goes to the Department of the Environment. The Department will send an inspector to hold a local enquiry into objections and to hear any claims that certain properties in the area have been well maintained and are, therefore, eligible for additional compensation payments: the sort of evidence heard at this type of enquiry will not be dissimilar from that presented to a county court judge adjudicating on a closing order. Inspectors hold other types of local enquiry, the most common are those arising out of refusals to agree to applications to develop land by building or extracting minerals. Other examples are enquiries into objections into the compulsory purchase of land by local authorities for housing, school-building, road-widening, etc., and disputes over footpaths. Save in minor planning cases, the inspector does not himself make the decision. His task is to listen to evidence presented by both sides to a dispute, normally to visit the site in question, and make a report with a recommendation to the appropriate Minister. The Minister is responsible for the final decision and in the vast majority of cases will uphold the inspector's opinion. Since 1958 the reports of inspectors have been published, unless considerations of national security are involved, so it is possible to see if the Minister has overruled his inspector.

Ministers also adjudicate in disputes between local authorities. Here there are no public enquiries; the councils concerned submit arguments on paper and the issue is decided within the Department. If education authorities are in dispute over which of them is responsible for the education of a child, the matter is determined by the Secretary of State for Education. If a similar issue arises over a child taken into care, responsibility is allocated by the Secretary of State for the Social Services. If a county council disagrees with a county district over whether a local plan is in conformity with the strategic county plan, the issue is referred to the Secretary of State for the Environment.

The remaining types of administrative control are all related to finance. Each new category of local authority created since 1844 has had to have its accounts examined by a government appointed auditor—now known as district auditor. Boroughs outside London were the only authorities to escape: they could choose between employing professional auditors, using district audit or choosing auditors by election—the latter method was quaintly archaic and rarely used. Except for London the 1972 Act permits councils to choose between district audit and professional audit, but an appointment in the latter category must be approved by the Secretary of State. Relatively few authorities took advantage of this new freedom. Only three counties and seven metropolitan districts use professional audit and half of these retain district audit to check some of their accounts. The district auditor must be satisfied that accounts are accurate and compiled in accordance with proper accounting principles. Any criticisms are to be included in his report to the local authority and the Secretary of State. Professional auditors report similarly. The Secretary of State may instruct the district auditor to hold an extra-ordinary audit into any accounts either as a result of local complaints or comment by a professional auditor. Penal powers of district audit are now supervised by the law courts and are considered in the following section.

Since local authorities obtain much financial aid from central government it is inevitable that these grants should form another means of central control. The nature of the control depends partly on the grant system. Where a grant is made for expenditure on a specific service, the way in which that service is developed can be greatly influenced by an alteration in the amount of the grant or by a change in the rules governing the eligibility of local expenditure to earn grant. Alternatively, the yardsticks which control the scale of expenditure on construction projects may be adjusted. In 1958 the number of local government functions which had a separate grant was reduced; central financial aid to the local rate fund is now largely distributed in the form of general grants not linked to expenditure on specific services. However, the general grant can exert much influence over the policy of local councils: if the grant is unexpectedly generous, councils will spend more freely, but if it does not increase as much as they hoped then there is encouragement to cut back their estimates. A reserve power also exists, never yet used, which enables the Government to refuse payment of the general grant to a local authority if the Government is gravely dissatisfied with the way in which the authority has been carrying out its duties.

The third category of financial control arises from control of local borrowing. When a local authority proposes to purchase or construct a capital asset which will be of benefit to the ratepayers in the future, the expenditure is normally financed by borrowing so that the cost of the asset can be spread over a number of years. Thus the need to obtain loan sanction is a powerful ministerial weapon. Originally, the requirement for loan sanction was imposed so that Ministers could ensure that local schemes were both reasonable in terms of local financial resources and were also technically sound.

This provided a safeguard for smaller authorities with less well qualified staff and enabled them to benefit from the wider experience of Ministry officials. Since 1939, however, the major purpose of this control has changed, for it has become a vital part of the general supervision which the Government exercises over the national economy. To this end, the total of capital expenditure allowed to all public authorities is fixed each year, and local authorities receive a ration from this amount. Thus local authorities have to fit into a national economic plan, and the amount of capital resources they are permitted to consume in any period will depend upon Government policy. Before 1979 capital expenditure financed other than by borrowing was not subject to central control. So money drawn from rate revenue reserve funds or sale of assets could be used without restraint. The Thatcher Government intends to extend control to cover all capital expenditure with a limited exception for revenue derived from the sale of assets. Approvals for expenditure are divided into five main blocks, education, housing, social services, transport and the rest. (Police spending is controlled separately.) The sum allocated to each block will then be distributed among local authorities, who will have to work within these ceilings. A little flexibility may be achieved by using part of the previous year's allocation that was not spent. Within a county there is also a limited provision for virement which means that an authority that does not need all its allocation for capital spending may pass some of it on to another council that finds its authorisation insufficient.

The wide scope of administrative control requires regular communications between local authorities and central departments. Applications from individual authorities are normally dealt with through correspondence. General guidance from Departments to local authorities comes through a variety of documents, some printed and some duplicated. Some bulletins deal with technical matters of concern to specialists. More general questions are dealt with in Circulars; the importance of Circulars has grown so considerably that they are commonly treated as an extra means of central control rather than simply as a method of communication. Their contents vary. Some seek to promote a particular course of action while others merely provide information. Before 1979 a file of these Circulars was a good guide to contemporary developments in local government. More recently the total of Circulars has been reduced as part of the Conservative desire for economy in administration.

A third means of communication is through personal contact.

When a council has a serious problem it may send a small deputation of councillors and officials to London to put their point of view to civil servants or perhaps even a Minister. Civil servants also visit local authorities, but such visits are most often made by officials with specialised qualifications, e.g. engineers, surveyors and planners. Senior civil servants, the members of the administrative class who have the greatest influence on Ministry decisions, more rarely travel round local authorities. This is a possible ground of criticism. It is arguable that central control would be more flexible, that central departments would have a fuller understanding of local difficulties, if there was more personal intercourse between Whitehall and the counties and districts. Yet it is not certain that local authorities would welcome more visits from civil servants. They are, quite rightly, jealous of their independence and would resent anything that seemed to be a call from a new type of general inspector.

The total of administrative controls is very great. No doubt, a case can be advanced for each item in the catalogue. The danger, of course, is that their cumulative impact can have a deadening effect on the whole of local government.

For decades the local authorities have expressed concern at the vast number of detailed controls to which they are subject. They greatly increase administrative cost. They hinder local initiative. They make for difficulties in adapting national policies to local circumstances. After years of grumbling the associations of local authorities ultimately took more positive action. In 1979 they produced a *Review of Central Government Controls over Local Authorities.* The report was detailed and revealed a bureaucratic nightmare. It showed that 227 different forms dealing with financial matters had to be completed. There were a further 30 questionnaires dealing with housing matters. Ministers had power to tell local councils how to control unruly bus queues or restrict the use of horses and carts. Apart from such trivia there was the more important complaint that government departments gave conflicting advice: the Treasury and the DOE counselled financial restraint while the DHSS issued guidelines which implied a need to expand services.

Mr Michael Heseltine, the new Conservative Secretary for the Environment, responded favourably to this document. It fitted well with the Conservative view that the business of government should be simplified and made cheaper. So many detailed controls disappeared. This does not mean that local authorities now have a much greater degree of freedom in any broad sense. The Conservative method is to mould the actions of local authorities by imposing financial restraint. A council that rebels against such discipline is forced into imposing a massive increase in the level of their rate and it may well stir indignation among local inhabitants which can affect local election results.

JUDICIAL CONTROL

Government departments had few personnel and resources before the second half of the nineteenth century. Administrative control of local government in the modern sense was unknown and impossible. County justices exercised somewhat erratic supervision over parish officers, but the justices themselves and the municipal corporations enjoyed a high degree of independence. The means of redress for a disgruntled citizen was to bring a legal action against a local authority. Thus judicial control formerly had an important effect on the development of local government. Today its effect is much reduced although certain legal principles inherited from the past still exert substantial influence.

A full discussion of the subject requires an extersive description of case law and the technicalities of legal procedure. This can be found in legal text-books and will not be attempted here. However, a brief analysis of their legal position is necessary for a complete understanding of the constitutional position of local authorities.

Local government law can be divided into two sections. There are branches of general law, e.g. contract and tort, where special rules apply in relation to local government. A local authority cannot be held liable on an *ultra vires* contract because it had no power to make the contract in the first place. In general, a local authority is responsible for the tortious—i.e. wrongful—acts of its servants. Since an authority has no power to commit torts one might expect, following the doctrine applied to contracts, that it could not be liable for wrongs done by its employees. Fortunately, in this instance, the courts have not been logical or consistent. However, there are exceptions to the general rule. If a local authority employee is acting under powers conferred on him personally by statute, the authority is not liable for his actions. Local authorities also have a wide range of powers that are not possessed by a private person, rights of entry into private premises for certain purposes, rights to destroy infected goods or unsound food, etc. It follows that many things done by local government officers, which would be tortious acts if undertaken by private individuals, are legitimated by statute.

The other sector of local government law relates specifically to the way in which local authorities carry out their functions. Here again a twofold distinction can be made between provisions for appeals against council decisions and wider opportunities for ensuring that local authorities both keep within their powers and carry out their duties.

Magistrates' courts deal with disputes arising out of the application of building regulations and the naming of streets. County courts hear appeals against closing orders. The High Court hears appeals against compulsory purchase orders and clearance orders. This is a selection of examples, not an exhaustive list. But it must be noted that the powers of the High Court to review compulsory purchase and similar orders are very limited: any action must be started within six weeks of the order being confirmed and the Court can consider an appeal only on grounds of *ultra vires* or if it is satisfied that the applicant has been 'substantially prejudiced' by some defect in the procedure when the order was being prepared and considered. The time limit is necessary to prevent local authorities being required to restore houses that have been knocked down or to return land to its previous owners after work has started on the erection of new buildings.

The sector of judicial control which offers the greatest constitutional interest is that relating to the extent of local authority powers and the way in which they are used. The principle of *ultra vires* has been described above. Here it may be useful to give an illustration of how closely the principle is applied. In *Attorney-General* v. *Fulham Corporation* (1921) the issue was whether Fulham Council had the power to run a municipal laundry. The Baths and Washhouses Acts, 1846-7, gave Fulham, as a public health authority, the right to provide baths and washhouses where people could wash themselves and wash clothes. The question was whether this power allowed Fulham to provide a service whereby the servants of the Council would wash clothes in return for payments to the Corporation. The Court's answer was 'no'. There have been many cases of this kind in which *ultra vires* has been used to obtain a ruling, often a restrictive ruling, on the meaning to be placed on words used in local government statutes. Judicial proceedings can also be instituted to force a local authority to carry out its statutory obligations: such a case would now be a rarity, but in previous centuries there have been important instances relating to the maintenance of highways and the provision of drainage.

Decisions by the District Auditor in relation to *ultra vires* acts are now wholly supervised by the courts. If the Auditor thinks that any item of expenditure is illegal, he may apply to the court for a declaration to that effect. Should the court agree with the Auditor, it may also impose a surcharge on any person responsible for illegal payments, except where it finds that an action was reasonable or taken in the belief that the expenditure was lawful. Where a councillor is surcharged more than £2,000 he can also be disqualified from membership of a local authority. Another possibility is that the examination of accounts may discover fraud. Here the Auditor can order the individual responsible to repay the sum involved; anyone aggrieved by such an order can appeal to the court.

Local authorities can also be required to observe certain rules of equitable behaviour known as the principles of 'natural justice'. The two most important are that no man shall be judge in his own cause and that no man shall be condemned unheard. If an elected member participates in the making of a decision of benefit to himself, then it can be declared void by a court. In 1933 a decision of the Hendon Rural District Council to permit the construction of a roadhouse was quashed because one of the councillors present was financially interested in the project. There are difficulties and limitations connected with these declarations of interest which will be discussed in Chapter VI. The other concept that no man shall be condemned unheard, has led to the establishment of a wide range of public enquiries into the actions of public authorities, especially where these are likely to interfere with private property and other rights. It also governs the way in which these enquiries are conducted. The leading case here is *Errington* v. *Ministry of Health* (1935). The facts were that the Minister of Health had ordered a public enquiry into objections against a clearance order made by a local authority. The enquiry was duly held by a Ministry inspector, but subsequently the inspector visited the site accompanied by local authority officials but without the objectors. This was held to constitute listening to evidence from one side in the absence of the other, so the High Court quashed the Minister's decision to confirm the clearance order. It will be noted that this was not an action against a local authority, but an action against the way in which a Minister had used his supervisory powers over local government.

An outstanding example of judicial control in recent years is the Tameside dispute of 1976. Tameside is a metropolitan district in Greater Manchester created by the Local Government Act, 1972. It is one of the three metropolitan districts not to contain a former county borough and so is a 'new' education authority in a real sense. The Labour majority on the council made arrangements to end selection for secondary schools in 1976 and to operate a comprehensive system. However, the Conservatives won the local election a few months before the changeover was due and they were pledged to retain some grammar schools. After some preliminary negotiations with Tameside, the Secretary of State, Mr Mulley, issued a direction that Tameside should give up the intention to continue selective entry to some secondary schools. This instruction was based on Section 68 of the Education Act, 1944, which provides that when the Secretary of State is satisfied that a local education authority is acting unreasonably a direction may be issued to that authority such as appears to the Secretary of State to be expedient. The language of the Act is so broad that one might have thought that Mr Mulley's action was fully justified, at least in law. Yet Tameside appealed to the courts. The case was fought up to the House of Lords where Mr Mulley lost.

Their Lordships held that there was no basis on which the Secretary of State was entitled to say that Tameside was acting unreasonably. They rejected the Whitehall view that plans for comprehensive education were so far advanced that it was impractical to change them and that the difficulties of arranging a selection system in the short time available were insuperable. There was, of course, a major political aspect of this conflict. A Bill then before Parliament, now the Education Act, 1976, required authorities not already operating on comprehensive principles to submit plans for ending selection. But the courts take no notice of Bills that have not reached the Statute Book.

In the past Section 68 had rarely been used to settle a major controversy; it has been used regularly in individual cases where parents have appealed to the DES against a local refusal to send a child to a particular school. So the Section had been used to uphold parental choice. Now its force is in doubt. Any dispute between a local education authority and the Secretary of State over what is reasonable may be referred to a court and there is clearly no guarantee that the ministerial direction will be supported. Thus the judgement of a Minister responsible to Parliament can be replaced by the judgement of judges responsible to no one.

If there is disagreement over the meaning of words in a statute it is proper that the matter be settled in a court of law. To this extent, judicial control over local government is unavoidable. It remains, however, an unsatisfactory process. Local authorities are responsible to the local electorate and try to serve the public interest as they think best. They are in a quite different position to the ordinary defendant in that they rarely break the law deliberately. If they do break the law, it is normally because a law is unclear or becomes unclear when lawyers start arguing about it. Another aspect of litigation is the heavy expense, so local authorities are not challenged in the courts—other than before the magistrates—unless someone is prepared to spend a substantial sum. It follows that judicial control is partial in its operation. Some parts of local government law have been heavily contested in the courts while other parts go unchallenged. The statutes that are disputed tend to be those that affect property, i.e. rating, housing, compulsory purchase and town and country planning. The Tameside case noted above is untypical in the sense that the amount of recent litigation over educational administration has been small.

The merit of being able to appeal to a Minister rather than a judge is cheapness. Yet we recoil from the idea that a Minister should be able to interpret the law for this would place still more power in ministerial hands. There may also be a feeling that, as a dominant factor in the sphere of public administration, a Minister would be biased in favour of local authorities against individuals, or would be guided by political considerations. A judge is held to be impartial and to give decisions based on recognised rules of statutory interpretation. However, since judges often find it possible to disagree, it is arguable that a judicial decision may be nothing more than the personal preference of a judge. Even so, the personal view of a judge may still be preferable to the personal view of a Minister in that a judicial decision can be overruled by subsequent parliamentary discussion and action, whereas a ministerial decision is virtually irreversible in Parliament because of party loyalty and party discipline.

Chapter V

FINANCE

THE SCALE OF OPERATIONS

Every benefit involves cost. Because local authorities organise a wide range of social provision, they consume a considerable fraction of the nation's resources of goods and manpower: it has reached about one-seventh of the gross domestic product. To put the matter in financial terms, local councils have an annual financial turnover of the order of £20,000 million. The spending and the collection of huge sums necessarily create a number of intricate problems.

A dominant feature of local finance is the meticulous care taken to control spending. Every authority prepares annually a detailed set of estimates to govern expenditure in the financial year starting on April 1st. Once approved by the council these estimates act as a check on subsequent expenditure. 'We cannot do anything about it this year because no provision has been made in the estimates' is a common explanation for failure to take action. Strict budgetary control is reinforced by auditing, by both internal and external auditors. Complicated rule systems have evolved to determine the legitimacy of expenditure. All this helps to prevent waste and corruption, although the auditing controls themselves cost a great deal of money.

In local finance a careful distinction is made between revenue expenditure and capital expenditure. Capital spending involves the purchase of an asset which will last for years to come. Thus money spent on school building or house building is of a capital nature while the money spent on an official's salary is not. The distinction is important because local authorities can borrow to defray the cost of capital items. Not all capital spending is financed by borrowing; many small items are charged against current income. Loans have to be repaid and the cost of loan repayment including interest charges is included in revenue expenditure; such costs constitute a high proportion of revenue expenditure on housing.

Above 60 per cent of current expenditure is now financed from central government grants. This overall figure conceals local variations because less prosperous areas enjoy levels of grant larger than the national average. The local rates withstand the highest proportion of expenditure in places where rateable values are high. Trading profits now make a negligible contribution to local resources. The Exchequer grants can be divided between the Rate Support Grant which, as the name implies, is a general subsidy to local government, and a number of grants in support of specific services, e.g. police and housing. The Rate Support Grant is by far the more important factor amounting to nearly 90 per cent of the total national aid. On the expenditure side, the most costly service is education which accounts for roughly half of all the outgoings. For this reason one of the most common remedies suggested to ease the burden of the rates is to transfer the cost of teachers' salaries to central government.

While the global sums involved in local finance are immense, the financial resources of individual councils vary greatly, although the largest disparities were eliminated by the 1972 reorganisation. Figures for the rateable values of major authorities will be found in the Appendix. It has been assumed in the past, rather too easily, that low rateable value damages the quality of local services. In fact, quality probably depends more on the opinions of councillors than on the details of the local financial situation. Some of the poorest authorities, judged by the standard of rateable value per head, have maintained an excellent standard; partly this has been due to the central grant system and partly to decisions by councillors to incur expenditure that would involve a high rate poundage in the belief that their electors would accept that the money spent was well spent.

Every local council has to bear full responsibility for its own expenditure—subject to assistance from the central government. However, some expenditure is 'pooled'. This applies in the case of a specialised service which would be uneconomic for each authority to organise. So the service is provided by a particular council or some other agency in return for payment by other local authorities. Such arrangements cover advanced further education, approved schools, the training of teachers and health visitors and 'no area' pupils, i.e. pupils who are not the responsibility of any particular local education authority. Various formulae determine the details of these pooling schemes. One difficulty is that the authority providing the service may have little incentive to economise since it may itself have to defray but a small part of total expenditure. The problem has now been recognised, in particular by the Department of Education and Science, and cost limits have been placed on pooled education expenditure.

In 1974 there was a major outburst of protest against rate increases as these reached levels previously unknown. Many authorities increased their rate demands by 50 per cent; a few extreme cases showed rises of nearly 100 per cent. This massive escalation of cost was caused by a unique combination of factors only partially related to local government reorganisation. Inflation and high interest rates were major influences on the rising tide of local expenditure. The Water Act, 1973, which transferred water and sewerage functions to the new Regional Water Authorities, was not an integral part of local government reform but it had a serious effect on rate levels. The water authorities obtain their revenue from a charge attached to local rates and the sums required were substantially higher than the product of the water and sewerage rates formerly levied by local authorities. All new bodies faced heavy expense in setting up their organisations. Reorganisation had a number of other more direct effects on expenditure. It encouraged improvements in local services. Authorities which were merged together often provided facilities of different quality. When these came to be evened out there was a natural tendency to adopt the better standard. Then reorganisation led to the employment of more local officials. Finally there were the more obvious costs of reorganisation related to the acquisition of new premises and equipment.

Again in 1980 there were large rate increases and consequent protests. On this occasion the reasons were partly different. The common feature was the continuing inflation which forced up salaries, wages and the prices of everything local authorities have to buy. But in 1980 the problem was aggravated by Conservative policy to reduce public expenditure, a policy which led to restrictions on the amount of central financial support for local councils. This adjustment helped the national taxpayer but forced up the rates.

It has now become apparent that the present basis of local taxation—the rate—is inadequate to meet the burden placed upon it. The implications of this statement are considered in the final section of this chapter.

THE RATING SYSTEM

It was noted in Chapter I that the Elizabethan Poor Law laid the foundation for the present rating system. As local services developed their cost was met by extra rates added on to the parish poor rate: thus county rates and school board rates were linked with the poor rate. Such charges were imposed on the whole country, both town and rural areas. Urban areas had further expenses, mainly connected with sanitary services under the Public Health Acts, which were financed by a separate rate collected in boroughs and urban districts. In these areas two separate rates were imposed. Many towns obtained powers to unify the collection of money, but this wasteful and stupid duplication was not finally ended until 1925. Under the 1972 reorganisation the districts and the London Boroughs levy the rate. Other authorities, the counties, the parishes and an assortment of joint boards with special powers, obtain income by precepting on the rating authorities. The level of the rate necessarily varies with local financial circumstances. Outside London it may vary within the area of a rating authority: in particular, wherever parish expenditure has to be added to the sums required to meet district and county expenses. In the non-metropolitan counties a very high proportion of rate revenue is handed on to the county councils because they are responsible for the most expensive services, notably education. The Layfield Report wanted to stop precepting so that the public became more conscious of the charges imposed by each local authority. It suggested that separate rate demands could be included in one envelope.

Liability to pay rates falls normally on the occupier of premises. Occupation is generally thought of in terms of control of the front door: a lodger does not control the front door and so is not liable. In some cases the owner of a property may be liable instead of the occupier(s). This applies to properties with a very low rateable value and to blocks of flats. Alternatively, an owner may come to an agreement with the rating authority to collect the rates from tenants along with the rents. For this trouble he receives a compounding allowance or discount from the rating authority. Until 1966, occupation was defined as beneficial occupation: no rates were payable on empty premises. However, rating authorities now have the option of imposing rates on premises unoccupied for three months, or six months in the case of new houses and flats. Many councils have decided not to exercise this power because a high proportion of the additional revenue could be consumed by the extra costs of collection. The Local Government Act, 1974, also gave power to impose a penal rating surcharge on unoccupied office property. Some property is excused from payment. Agricultural land has been exempt since 1929. Crown land is also exempt; in practice, the Treasury makes an equivalent contribution. Property used for or in connection with religious worship, public parks, sewers, lighthouses, buoys, beacons, sheds for housing invalid chairs, and the residences of ambassadors and their servants, are also exempt; and so are certain classes of machinery not deemed to be part of a building. Almshouses and other properties used for charitable purposes enjoy a 50 per cent reduction in the amount of rates payable, and rating authorities have a discretionary power to remit their rates altogether. This discretionary power to reduce or remit rates extends to other nonprofit making institutions, e.g. social clubs and educational, literary and scientific bodies.

The Rating Act, 1966, was designed to ease the situation of rate-payers with low incomes. It authorised collection by instalments and provided for remission of rates for poorer persons not in receipt of national assistance. Each applicant for a rebate has to submit to a means test and the amount of relief granted depends upon a scale which is adjusted from time to time, to take account of changes in the value of money. Ninety per cent of the cost of these concessions is met by a government grant. In fact, fewer people have applied for rebates than was initially anticipated. Considerable pressure of claims arises in seaside towns where there are many elderly persons in receipt of fixed incomes often living in quite expensive properties.

How much is a ratepayer required to pay? This depends on two factors—the valuation placed on his property (the technical term is hereditament) and the poundage levied by the local rating authority. To give a simple example: if a house has a net assessment of £400 and the poundage charged is 75p, the liability for the year will be £300. It follows that valuation of properties for rating purposes is a matter of financial concern to every ratepayer. The valuation is an attempt to define the annual value of a hereditament. While all rating valuation is based on this single principle, various means are used to arrive at the assessment in relation to different classes of property. However, shops and houses are assessed on the basis of a reasonable rent for the property; this figure is known as the Gross Annual Value. There is a standard scale of allowances to cover maintenance and insurance costs which are deducted from the Gross Value and this produces a second and lower figure, the Net Annual Value, on which rates are actually paid. Other techniques of assessment are used for factories, licensed premises and nationalised industries.

The task of valuation has been carried out by the Inland Revenue since 1948. Originally, of course, it was the duty of the overseer. Through the years various checks had to be imposed on the overseers to try to ensure that they did not undervalue property in their parish. There was substantial advantage to be gained from undervaluation in relation to charges assessed over a wider area than the parish, e.g. the district or county, because lower valuation allowed a parish to escape with paying a lower share of the total costs. The Rating and Valuation Act, 1925, abolished overseers and transferred the valuation function to county boroughs and area valuation committees which covered a group of neighbouring county districts. Finally the system was nationalised in 1948 to achieve uniformity. As a new system of government grants was introduced at this time designed to give greatest aid to authorities with the lowest rateable values per head of population, this uniformity was essential to ensure fairness in the distribution of the grant. In these circumstances the inducement to undervalue property would have been very strong. The first valuation list produced on a national basis became effective in 1956. It showed conclusively that the earlier standards of assessment must have been extremely varied. To take the extreme examples: in 1956 the rateable value of Radnor was increased by 17 per cent, but nearby in Cardigan rateable value of the county went up by 160 per cent. Cardigan had been under assessed before while Radnor valuations had been very much higher. In theory, a completely new valuation list is produced every five years, but they tend to be postponed. The 1961 revaluation was put off until 1963; the 1968 valuation was put back to 1973; the revision due in 1978 has again been further postponed until 1980. However, valuation of particular properties may be altered at any time to take account of extensions or improvements: by the Local Government Act, 1974, alterations are not to be made in respect of minor structural alterations.

Any ratepayer may appeal against an assessment and argue his case before a local valuation court. A further appeal from a decision of this body can be made to the Lands Tribunal. To succeed an appeal must show that there is some injustice in the valuation. It is useless to go before the valuation court and say that you cannot afford to pay so much in rates. But if it can be shown that similar properties have a lower assessment, or that more desirable properties have the same assessment, or that the value of a property has been adversely affected by some local development, then an appeal can succeed.

In 1929 when agricultural land was derated altogether, industrial and freight-transport hereditaments were also relieved of three-quarters of their rate liability. But since the war the law on valuation for rating has been changed frequently in response to political and administrative pressures. In the 1963 valuation list the derating of industrial and freight-transport hereditaments was ended (Rating and Valuation Act, 1961). Dwelling-houses, shops and offices are now rated also on current values, so there have been drastic upward adjustments everywhere in the assessments of residential property. Of course, the rate paid by the residential occupier does not increase *pro rata* with a rise in assessments because the rise in total rateable values, including the greater amounts accruing from industrial premises, should permit broadly equivalent reductions in the level of the rate poundage. But any ratepayer will suffer if his own assessment has risen proportionately more than the average of assessments in his area. The rate burden also tends steadily to increase as local authorities are forced to pass on the rising charges for goods and services which they require.

The rating of nationalised industries presents a special problem; their physical assets are not Crown property but are assessable to rates. Three of them, the railways, the gas industry and the electricity supply industry, have fixed plant obviously not self-contained in any rating areas. Special arrangements operate under the General Rate Act, 1967, for the ascertainment of the total rateable value of such assets in the areas of the owning Boards and the apportionment of the rate liabilities in respect of them among the rating authorities.

We now turn from valuation to the calculation of the rate poundage. The local financial year starts on April 1st, so in January and February estimates are prepared of spending in the coming financial year; these will be considered by a finance or central policy committee, possibly pruned back, and presented to the council for final approval. The detailed work is carried on by the Treasurer and his staff in consultation with the other spending committees. Obviously this involves pre-planning of future activities and requires important policy decisions to be made, so the preparation of estimates can be both a complex and controversial exercise. The final total of projected expenditure is a major feature of the local budget, but there are other factors which affect the extent of the demands made on ratepayers—national grants, local revenue from rents, fees and other charges and unspent balances, if any, from the previous year. A local authority is not entitled to accumulate surpluses on revenue account, so if expenditure in any one year is less than estimated the saving should be devoted to reducing the rate levy in the following year. Of course, an adequate working balance is permitted and a margin for unexpected contingencies.

When the figures for the various parts of the budget are available, the size of the gap between expenditure and non-rate revenue becomes apparent. This is the gap that has to be filled by local taxation. If the charge on the rate fund shows a steep rise on the previous year, there may well be demands for reductions in expenditure. The rate poundage is fixed by relating the income required from the rate to the rateable value of a local authority's domain; the latter is the sum of the net rateable values of all properties in the area. Thus if a council has a rateable value of £5,000,000 and requires to raise three-quarters of this sum, the probable rate levy is 76p in the £—the extra penny being required to cover contingencies and the loss of revenue on empty property, various remissions and bad debts. This is, naturally, a greatly simplified picture of the local budgetary process; in reality, the calculations involved are highly complex. One other concept must be noticed, that of the penny rate product which is the amount produced by imposing a rate of a penny in the pound and equals one-hundredth of the local rateable value, ignoring the effect of empty property. The penny rate product is a useful way of showing the cost of any new policy. To revert to the earlier example, an authority with a rateable value of £5,000,000 has a penny rate worth £50,000, so that a £100,000 scheme that earned no revenue of its own and attracted no national grant would cost a twopenny rate.

Until 1967 all classes of ratepayers paid the same rate in the pound. There had been, as was noted above, many shifts and adjustments in the methods of assessing various types of property, but at least the rate poundage was uniform. Now valuation is tolerably uniform but rate poundage varies because the domestic ratepayer is allowed to pay at a lower figure than other categories of ratepayer. This development is discussed more fully below.

GOVERNMENT GRANTS

When the state required local government to undertake new duties it often made a grant in aid of the new service to ease the financial burden. Alternatively, grants were given to reduce the cost of an activity obviously of national as well as local benefit; a clear example is the grant made to meet the cost of criminal prosecutions in 1834. There is, of course, room for argument over which services are of national benefit. Public health is of national interest because disease can spread across local authority boundaries. An efficient police force is of national benefit whereas a local playing field is not. Through the years views have changed on the nature and extent of the public interest and the term is now given a much wider definition than in the nineteenth century. The Victorian controversy about the exact distinction between what were described as local beneficial services and national onerous services deserving national aid now seems curiously antique. However, this distinction had an important role in the evolution of the grant system. Grants were also given to ease the burdens of the poorer areas and to ensure that minimum standards were maintained over services thought to be of national importance. Financial recompense also has had to be made to local councils when the national government reduces their taxing powers, e.g. the derating of agricultural land and the partial derating of industry in 1929 and the domestic rate relief imposed by the Local Government Act, 1966.

There has been a succession of changes in government financial policy towards local authorities. Various types of grant have been used. The main distinction is between specific grants and general grants. The specific grant is given to aid a particular local service and is usually given on a percentage basis. An alternative is a unit basis—so much per house or flat. The percentage arrangement has two disadvantages. It may encourage extravagant spending, especially if the percentage grant is high: where a 50 per cent grant applies, the local authority can expect to recover half its expenditure. In consequence, central departments have to impose some check on local expenditure, probably by setting down categories of spending that will be accepted for grant purposes. This involves more central supervision of local government and an increase in administrative cost.

The general grant is a contribution to local rate funds not tied in this way. Again, it can take one of two main forms; either it can be designed specifically to help the poorest authorities or it can be given to all councils. Distribution is governed by a formula which will either try to assess the poverty of an area or will assess need by reference to the size and nature of the population. A general grant is simpler administratively. Arguably it is more conducive to local independence and freedom from central supervision. It also encourages good housekeeping by local authorities. The amount of grant is fixed before the start of a financial year so the councils know in advance their income from the Government. Any extra sums they may be tempted to spend fall squarely on the rates. Quite naturally, the general grants method has always been preferred by the Treasury. Essentially the history of the grant system over the past hundred years is one of continuous growth but also of ebb and flow between the general and specific categories. In 1888, 1929 and again in 1958 many specific grants were swept away and replaced by (more) general grants. The education grant disappeared in 1958. Critics claimed that its termination would lead to cuts in the standards of educational provision, but this did not happen because the increase in the general subvention was more than adequate to compensate for the termination of the separate education grant. The Labour Opposition was highly critical of the 1958 decision; however, when in office they did not reverse it. Indeed, speaking on the 1966 Local Government Bill in the House of Commons, Mr Crossman laid down two criteria for specific grants, that there must be a need to control the service centrally or that the expenditure involved must be distributed unevenly between authorities. The police are an example of the first and coast protection of the second.

The main specific grants now in operation are for housing, police and transport. The Local Government Act, 1974, introduced a new transport supplementary grant (TSG) the amount of which is negotiated alongside the annual discussions on the size of the general grant—now termed the Rate Support Grant. Transport grants are related to local expenditure on highways, public transport subsidies and traffic regulation. To explain and justify their spending programmes each county council has to submit to central government a document entitled Transport Policy and Programme (TPP) which contains a statement of transport objectives and strategy over the next decade or so. The TSG/TPP system is a clear example of the strong link between specific grants and central control; in 1977 the transport grant for South Yorkshire was cut drastically because the Government opposed the local policy of providing large subsidies to keep down the level of bus fares.

The Local Government Act, 1974, also provided that central government would meet 90 per cent of the cost of awards to students at universities and teacher training colleges or following courses of equivalent standard. The Layfield Report was notably unenthusiastic about specific grants. It urges that the whole costs of mandatory student awards be met by the government and that police and transport grants be merged into the Rate Support Grant.

General grants commenced their tortuous history with the assigned revenues of 1888, the failure of which was noted in the introductory chapter. During and after the First World War a variety of new grants was made available to assist particular services. The Conservative Government, with Winston Churchill as Chancellor of the Exchequer, decided to reorganise methods of central financial aid and as from 1929 all specific grants were replaced with a general grant, apart from those for education, police, housing, certain health functions and roads in county areas.

The post-war Labour Government favoured specific grants which were increased in range and amount. The 1929 general grant was replaced in 1948 by the Exchequer Equalisation Grant which gave aid solely to the poorer authorities. This system lasted for ten years until in 1958 the Conservatives decided on another slaughter of specific grants, this time to include education. The Exchequer Equalisation Grant to help poorer districts was continued in a slightly modified form and renamed the Rate Deficiency Grant.

The present form of the general grant is the Rate Support Grant introduced initially in 1966. The size of the grant is determined by the Government in the light of current prices and costs and what it is felt the country can afford. The domestic element, explained below, is deducted from the total sum and the remainder, the block element, is distributed to local authorities in accordance with their population and resources. The RSG now constitutes about 90 per cent of central aid to local government.

When first introduced the domestic element gave residential

occupiers a fivepenny (approximately 2.1 new pence) reduction in 1967-8. The size of the reduction has increased steadily and by 1977 was 18.5p in England and 36p in Wales. Initially the domestic element was intended as a temporary palliative to minimise the harshness of the rating system until a more radical reform of local government finance could be undertaken. In 1979–80 the domestic element cost £725 million, a dramatic increase over the total of £30 million in 1967–68.

Complex annual discussions are held to determine the size of the rate support grant. Representatives of central government, and of local government, the latter nominated by the associations of local authorities, examine estimates of future expenditure in great detail. Since 1975 these discussions have been placed on a more formal level by the establishment of a Consultative Council on Local Government Finance which provides a useful forum for an exchange of views between Ministers and leading councillors. However, the Government retains the whip hand in these discussions both because it is providing the money and because local expenditure is now so large that it must be made to conform with the economic policy of the Cabinet. Since 1977 rates have had to bear a markedly increased proportion of local expenditure as a contribution towards solving our national economic difficulties. Negotiations over the RSG involve two main issues—the size of the grant and its distribution between authorities. The first question is linked directly to government economic policy and is the subject of an annual parliamentary debate. In a period of economic stringency, the RSG arouses much public interest. The second issue often causes a bitter wrangle between the associations of local authorities, particularly between the Association of County Councils and the Association of Metropolitan Authorities. These bodies make competing claims about hardships suffered in their areas. The AMA stress the problems of decaying inner city areas: the ACC stress the expense of providing services in rural conditions. After 1974 the Labour Government changed the basis of allocation to help the cities, but the Conservatives are more sympathetic to the shire counties so the tendency has been reversed.

At present, however, if some councils spend more than Ministers wish, financial discipline can be imposed only by reducing the total sum allocated to the RSG: when this is distributed according to formula, the councils which accepted the official guidelines suffer as well as the malefactors. The good boys are punished along with the bad. So the Government may well decide to replace the needs and resources elements of the RSG by a unitary grant to be calculated separately for each authority. The amount would be sufficient to bridge the gap between the cost of providing services comparable with those of similar authorities and the receipts from the local rate assuming it was fixed at a particular level specified by the central government. Thus Ministers would determine acceptable standards. Should a council wish to exceed these standards it could do so by increasing the local rate.

CAPITAL EXPENDITURE

Local authorities may borrow money to meet the cost of capital expenditure, subject to the consent of the Department of the Environment. Each loan has to be paid back over a period of years, the length of the period depending on the durability of the asset. The lifespan of capital assets is estimated on a conservative basis for this purpose; for example, loans for baths and wash-houses must be repaid over 30 years, for houses over 60 years, for housing land over 80 years. It follows that at the end of these periods the local authority will have a debt-free asset; it may achieve this position even earlier for no council is compelled to borrow for the maximum permissible period.

Inevitably, this raises the question—is it a good policy to borrow at all? An individual with an adequate income but no capital who seeks to buy a house has no alternative: he must try to borrow by raising a mortgage. But a local authority is not in the same situation. It has a flexible source of revenue and can increase its income by raising the rate poundage. Should ratepayers be forced to pay for capital assets immediately, without recourse to borrowing? This policy has one great advantage—cheapness. To raise a loan for a period as long as 60 years is extremely expensive. Interest rates are now very high. At the time of writing local authorities are having to pay 13 per cent. (Of course, if the rate of interest is below the rate of inflation, the lender stands to lose—quite apart from the tax that has to be paid on the interest received.) So local authorities can save money by paying for capital assets out of revenue, and a few councils did so in relation to at least part of their capital expenditure until the last war. Now the policy is out of favour for at least three reasons. Durable assets will be of benefit to the next generation of ratepayers, so why should the whole cost be met by the ratepayers of today? This is a powerful argument which is reinforced by the continuous tendency for the purchasing power of the pound to decline. A pound borrowed now will buy much more than it will when repaid in, say, fifty years time; admittedly this is only a prediction but all economic experience suggests it is a safe one! The faster the depreciation of currency, the greater the advantage to the debtor, the greater the loss to the creditor. The advantage to the debtor is offset by the interest that has to be paid but, unless interest rates are high, there is potential advantage in borrowing. At present interest rates are high, very high, and this encourages many authorities to charge small capital items to current revenue. To charge large capital sums to the rate fund would involve raising rate levels even more steeply and this would be politically unacceptable. If major capital schemes were financed from revenue, there is a danger that standards of provision would become not merely economical but parsimonious.

Ministerial control over local borrowing was firmly established by the end of the nineteenth century. The reasons for control of borrowing have changed over the years. Originally, the concern was to ensure that local authorities were not overstepping the limits of their financial resources by incurring unduly heavy commitments for the future repayment of debt. Such Gladstonian prudence has now gone. The central government was also concerned to ensure that engineering proposals by local authorities were technically sound: smaller authorities with inadequate specialist advice had to be protected from the possibility of expensive mistakes. Now the main task is to ensure that capital spending by local authorities is in conformity with the Government's overall economic programme and, indeed, is in conformity with Ministers' patterns of priorities. In any balance of payments crisis, the order is likely to come from Whitehall —no more town halls or swimming baths until the national economic situation improves: if the crucial problem is unemployment, then local authorities may be encouraged to spend more, e.g. on highway improvements.

Capital construction schemes are now allocated priorities two or three years in advance. To save administrative work loan sanction may be given not for individual projects but for a whole programme of construction. Once ministerial permission to borrow has been obtained, a local authority—and its Treasurer—are faced with two interrelated problems, how to obtain the loan and whether it is preferable to borrow on a short-term or long-term basis. The latter question involves attempting to forecast the future pattern of interest rates. If they are expected to rise, it is better to arrange a long-term loan with a fixed interest: if a fall is anticipated, it is better to arrange a short period loan so that the money can be reborrowed subsequently at a lower interest charge. From time to time the Treasury has expressed concern over the pattern of local authority debt. It has been worried that loan periods are too short. Local financial officers, hoping that interest rates will fall, have tended to opt for short-term borrowing. However, this policy creates a need for incessant re-borrowing, increases the instability of the capital market, creates a greater likelihood of default and magnifies the impact of changes in interest rates on local finances. A voluntary code of practice has been agreed between local authorities and the Government which will have the effect of steadily lengthening the average period of loans. Central super-vision over local borrowing has also been strengthened to control the amount of capital expenditure within a given financial year. Previously the loan sanction arrangements had been related to projects or programmes and did not determine dates within which the sanction could be used. Thus the capital schemes of local councils are forced to fit in with the Government's annual plans for public expenditure and become a buttress of national economic policy.

Various techniques of raising capital are available to a local authority. One is the Public Works Loan Board, established under an Act of 1875. The Board is financed by Government loans and the Treasury prescribes the interest rates to be charged. In recent years there have been a number of shifts of Government policy in relation to the PWLB. Originally the idea was that the Board should assist mainly the smaller authorities which lacked both the prestige and experience to raise funds easily in the money market. The tendency is still for the smaller authorities and those in less prosperous areas to make greatest use of the PWLB. The flow of capital through the Board remains well below the 50 per cent limit as some authorities find that they can borrow elsewhere on rather more favourable terms.

Other techniques of borrowing can be described briefly. Subject to Treasury consent, local authorities can issue stock. Relatively large sums of money can be obtained by this means for a long period and these advantages are important to large authorities when interest rates are not too high. The most common methods are to issue mort-gages or bonds. For technical reasons the bonds are simpler to administer and so are coming more into favour. Some capital is available from internal sources, e.g. superannuation funds. Short period and temporary loans are raised through the money market or from banks.

A general picture of local authority indebtedness can be obtained from the figures published by the Chartered Institute of Public Finance and Accountancy which show how capital debt has been utilised and the source of borrowing.

ANALYSIS OF LOCAL AUTHORITY DEBT, 1978

by service	£000,000	by form of debt	%
Housing:		Stock	5·4
Buildings, sites	18,595	Bonds and mortgages	30·6
Loans, improvement grants	3,469	PWLB	38·1
Education	3,859	Temporary loans	11·3
Highways	1,286	Internal advances	2·0
Trading services	617	Revenue	10·4
Town and Country Planning	889	Other	2·2
Amenity and Recreation	616		
Social Services	489		
Police and Fire	243		
Environmental Protection	193		
Other	1,201		
Total	31,457		

Source: CIPFA: *Summary of Debt Outstanding*

What role should the Government play in relation to local borrowing? Two views on this issue emerge in the local authority world. There is a general desire to remain as independent as possible of central control. There is also a feeling that, as most local loans are required to carry through national programmes, the Government should facilitate borrowing and perhaps offer favourable interest rates. Some advantages would accrue from the establishment of a central organisation to arrange a capital flow. The Institute of Municipal Treasurers and Accountants—now the Chartered Institute of Public Finance and Accountancy—has urged the establishment of such an agency which would have power to borrow on its own account, although it might be partly financed through the Consolidated Fund. This agency would not provide all loan capital required by local authorities which would continue to exercise initiative in fund raising. The scheme thus combines the attractions of local independence and central co-ordination. On the Government side there seems also to be two attitudes which ebb and flow. One stresses the need for a co-ordinated borrowing policy; the other wishes to avoid the strain on national borrowing facilities which would be imposed by an acceptance of full responsibility for local finance. There is no doubt that councils can tap funds from local sources that might not be available to the Government and many authorities can manage at present without making use of the PWLB. The problem is not lack of available capital, but high interest rates which are caused by national and international factors—not by the actions of local government.

RATES—INADEQUATE AND UNFAIR?

Rates probably cause more irritation than any other form of taxation. Before examining the causes of this discontent, it is well to look at the few advantages that can be claimed for the rates. The rating mechanism, in spite of complexities of detail, is traditional and is well understood. Now assessment has been nationalised, the valuations are generally just and, in any case, can be challenged by appeals. Since rates are payable on visible and immovable property, it is impossible to avoid paying. This means that the local authorities have a stable and reliable source of revenue. Rates are also a flexible tax in that it is easy to alter the level of the poundage. They are also economical to collect: according to the County Councils Association the collection cost is 1.2 per cent of the total revenue. Since rates are a tax on housing they act as a deterrent to under-occupation of property and may encourage people with excess accommodation to sub-let or move. And as the rates are imposed by local authorities they provide a degree of financial independence from the central government; without such independence, local councils would soon become mere agents of central departments spending from national funds. This last item in the catalogue is not an argument for rates *per se*, but it is an argument of basic importance for the retention by local authorities of an independent taxing capacity. So far no alternative to the rates has appeared to be politically or administratively acceptable; in these circumstances, the rates remain a bulwark of local autonomy.

Why then do rates provoke criticism? The first answer is psychological. Rates are a very obvious tax. Indirect taxes, for example those on tobacco, beer and petrol, are linked with the natural cost of the commodity: the public is generally aware that there is a substantial tax element in the total price, but the price is still accepted as the price *of the commodity*. Anyone entering a tobacconist's shop is not dominated by the thought that he is about to make a contribution to national revenue. Income tax, for the most part, is collected on a 'pay as you earn' basis, so the wage and salary earner comes to accept the net amount of his weekly or monthly pay-slip as his true income. The tax and insurance deductions are accepted, no doubt regretted, but ignored when it comes to planning personal expenditure. You do not miss what you have never had. In contrast to PAYE and indirect taxes, the rates are not hidden in any way. Money has to be extracted from disposable income and paid to the rates office. Since rates are usually payable on a half-yearly basis, the sum involved on each occasion is substantial: however, authorities are now less unwilling to collect by more frequent instalments. Yet it still remains true that ratepayers are more conscious of rates than of other forms of taxation. Other people may not share this awareness. And this is important because in 1945 when universal suffrage was extended to local government, a substantial gap developed between the number of people paying rates and those who can vote for councillors who impose rates. Those who suffer financial responsibility no longer correspond with those who exercise constitutional power. But this distinction should not be overstressed. Local authorities now obtain more revenue from grants than they do from the local rate and everyone is liable to contribute to national taxes. Further, adult members of a household normally contribute to its expenses and rent for furnished accommodation should contain a rate element.

There are many other objections. From the point of view of the local authority, the rates have an unsatisfactory tax base. Prices and costs rise ceaselessly; property values also rise but the quinquennial valuations are always postponed so that rateable values do not keep pace with the fall in the purchasing power of money. This means that rate poundages are forced up almost every year, thus creating annual discontent. It is also arguable that the reasonable rent basis of valuation for domestic property is largely spurious because, owing to the operation of rent restriction legislation, in many areas there is no free market in rented property. More equitable assessments might be achieved if capital values were used instead of hypothetical rental values. Householders may be deterred from expanding or improving their properties since to do so involves a bigger rate liability. There is also no connection between the use a ratepayer makes of local services and the extent of his rate bill. Whether this is a valid objection is a matter of opinion. Personal demands upon local services are either a matter of choice or need and, in so far as they result from need, the rate-supported services contribute to social equality. It is certain that areas in which the need for social welfare provision is greatest have the lowest rateable values per head; *vice versa* where needs are less, rateable values are high. This creates a situation in which it is easiest to raise rate revenue where it is least required as high rateable values tend to produce low rate poundages. The system of government grants is designed to assist the poorer areas, but they do not entirely eliminate disparities.

All this makes up a powerful case against rates. Yet the main criticism is that they fall unevenly on different classes of ratepayer. Those who are liable to pay in relation to shop, commercial and industrial premises can use their rate bill as an expense for which an allowance is made in relation to income tax liability. No such relief is available for the domestic ratepayer. Indeed, it is arguable that to give income tax relief for rate liability would be unfair since it would give no aid to those who need it most—those too poor to pay income-tax. In 1963 there was a great outcry about the unfairness of rating after the new valuation list had reassessed residential properties at current values. The storm of protest forced the Government to appoint a Committee to enquire into the impact of local rates on households. This Committee, under the chairmanship of Professor Allen, issued its report in 1965 and demonstrated clearly the regressive nature of local rates. Their incidence is quite different to income tax. A man with a large family enjoys substantial allowances in respect of his children when income tax is computed. He also needs to occupy more residential accommodation if he can afford it—and this will make him liable to pay more rates. A lodger pays no rates at all, at least directly. When the rating system was instituted on a national scale in 1601 it was broadly fair as between individuals since it was based on visible wealth, and the squire in the manor house could obviously afford to pay more than the tenant farmer or the yeoman. Today the size of a property is an unsure guide to the wealth of its occupants and their ability to contribute to the cost of local services.

However, the situation has altered dramatically since 1965. The Layfield Report showed that in 1975 households with a weekly income below £20 made no net contribution to the rates; above £20 a week the rates have a slowly increasing impact until a plateau is reached at income levels between £35 and £80 a week when the rates claimed between 2 per cent and 3 per cent of income; above £80 a week the rate demand consumes a diminishing proportion of income. So the regressive effect of local rates has been substantially diminished. Three factors have contributed to the change. More generous supplementary benefits have assisted low income groups to pay their rates. The Rating Act, 1966, provided for remission of rates for the poorest sections of the community, subject to a means test. The Local Government Act 1966, introduced a national subsidy to enable lower rates to be charged on all residential properties. This benefit is not subject to any income limitation and, as shown above, has been increased substantially over the years. Thus a great deal has been done to mitigate the hardships caused by the rating system but, because public memory is short, the extent of the improvement tends to be forgotten. Meanwhile, the policy of rate relief has one serious drawback—local government tends to become more financially dependent on the national Exchequer. And, inevitably, he who pays the piper calls the tune.

Local government would be greatly strengthened if it were given a stronger independent tax base. This thought was central to the Layfield Report but its recommendations had little effect. No action has been taken on the proposal that property be assessed on the basis of capital value rather than annual value. Another Layfield suggestion, to abolish agricultural derating, has been officially rejected. Such adjustments would strengthen the rating system but they do not really get to the heart of the problem. A satisfactory solution demands a new base for local taxation. Motor taxation duties might be transferred to local authorities. But if the *level* of charge were to be fixed locally, then it would be cheaper to register vehicles in some places than others: it might well become economic to garage large lorry fleets in areas with lower duties. Yet if the level of tax is not a matter for local decision, councils have no control over their income. A sales tax is more obviously capable of local adjustment, but it faces three major objections. Presumably it would be in addition to the national VAT and obviously would be a most unwelcome addition. Like the rates it would be regressive in that, unless restricted to luxury and semi-luxury goods, the burden would be heaviest on the poorest members of the community. Finally, people living in the countryside and in small towns spend money in bigger towns. To take the extreme case, London is almost a national shopping centre. So if the tax were collected by the present rating authorities on turnover in their own districts, rural areas would suffer badly. Were local government organised on a regional basis, this obstacle would partly disappear.

The idea of a local income tax has been widely canvassed for many years. It would add greatly to the financial independence of local government. As compared with a rate on property, it has the advantage that more people would be required to contribute to local revenues. The sums paid by individuals might also be more fairly related to their ability to pay; whether those with low incomes would benefit depends on the rules adopted for rate rebates and income tax relief. The Layfield Report, *Local Government Finance* (Cmnd 6453), published in 1976, suggested that local income tax should supplement local rates. It should be levied by local authorities that face the highest expenditure, the shire counties, the metropolitan districts and the London boroughs. However, the Layfield Report listed many practical difficulties to be faced. Expense is a serious obstacle. Rather than establish new local income tax offices, it would be cheaper to use the services of the Inland Revenue: however, the methods of the Revenue would need adjustment since income tax collection is based on the location of employers not on the residence of employees. Another problem is that at present national taxes are uniform; local income tax requires collection at varied levels. By the use of the Inland Revenue, Layfield estimated that administrative costs could be kept down to £100 million per annum at 1975 prices. Whether the advantages of the system justify such an amount is a matter of opinion, particularly when the trend of government policy is to restrict public expenditure.

Not surprisingly the Government's Green Paper issued in response to the Layfield Report (Cmnd 6813) rejected local income tax. The Treasury could be expected to resist any interference by local government with a key regulator of the economy. The Green Paper commented that local freedom 'to vary the LIT rate would have to be closely constrained so that it did not unduly complicate central government economic and financial management'. And if LIT were absorbed in PAYE deductions, the public would tend to lose sight of it; local accountability, so heavily emphasised by Layfield, would be lost.

It must be stressed that the Layfield support for local income tax was hedged by the stipulation that it should be linked with 'express moves towards giving greater power of decision to local authorities'. So the proposed reform was specifically associated with the wider question of relations between central and local government. This aspect of the Layfield Report is considered in Chapter X.

In the 1970s local government services expanded at a faster rate than the growth of the national economy. It followed that rate revenue had to increase not merely in monetary terms but as a proportion of the national product unless one of four other possibilities was adopted. These were a reduction in the scale of growth of local services; higher levels of central government grants; removal of some services from the ambit of local government; the development of other sources of revenue for local authorities. The first alternative slows down progress; the second implies loss of independence; the third weakens local government by limiting its scope. Clearly the fourth solution is the most acceptable to local authorities. In practice, the second and third alternatives were followed.

The arrival of the Thatcher Government produced a marked change of emphasis: the first and fourth alternatives have come to the fore. No longer is there a prospect of expanding local services. The argument has changed to one about cuts, how big they should be and where should they fall. Since the cuts adversely affect local authority staff and those who appreciate the benefits derived from local services, the arguments are vigorous. The fourth alternative to higher rates, other sources of local revenue, has also been pursued but in the context of more charges for local services rather than schemes for new forms of taxation. Conservative philosophy seeks a reduction in public expediture achieved partly by withholding benefits from those

110 THE REFORMED LOCAL GOVERNMENT SYSTEM

who can afford to do without them. Accordingly the Government intends to allow local authorities to charge for school transport and to raise the price of school meals to cover the full cost. Other charges, notably council house rents, are steadily increased. Restrictions on transport grants have an impact on bus services. Another means of increasing local revenue is to sell assets: the Conservatives favour the sale of council houses. Leaving aside the social consequences of this policy, it is a matter for argument whether the sale of capital assets at discount prices really helps the financial state of local councils. But the Conservatives yearn for a fuller acceptance of a private enterprise, free-market economy and, perforce, the financial affairs of local authorities are manipulated towards achieving this aim.

There remains the question of the future of the rating system. Certainly, the Conservatives are aware of its limitations. Their election manifesto in October, 1974, stated '. . . within the normal lifetime of a Parliament we shall abolish the domestic rating system and replace it by taxes more broadly based and related to people's ability to pay. Local authorities must continue to have some independent source of finance.' However, in 1979 the Party's manifesto was more cautious. It noted '. . . cutting income tax must take priority for the time being over abolition of the domestic rating system.' So the rates are reprieved and may well be with us for many years to come.

Chapter VI

PERSONNEL AND PROCEDURE

A local authority, like any other piece of state mechanism, is governed by both law and practice. The conventions that develop within the formal structure of a local authority have a great effect on the way in which business is carried through and how decisions are made. No systematic description of the arrangements is possible since they vary between each authority. There is, however, one dominating factor—the extent to which a council is influenced by the political loyalties of elected members. The importance of political parties in framing the conventions of public life can scarely be exaggerated. The work of a local authority is based on the interrelationships of officials and elected representatives working together through a committee system. Especially in urban areas the outcome is substantially affected by party activity. To ignore the effect of politics on local government is unrealistic and misleading: a broad description of the political setting must be given before we move on to consider the respective roles of officers and councillors.

THE IMPACT OF POLITICS

It is often argued that politics should have no place in local government. Certainly, there are some grounds for this view. Where elections are held on a party basis, no candidate other than those sponsored by a party has a real chance of success. Where one party is dominant in a particular ward or district, nomination by that party is tantamount to election to the local council, for electors become accustomed to voting on party lines and do not know, or do not care about, the qualities of the individual candidate. Attachment to a political party thus becomes an essential pre-condition of election to a local council; in so far as this limits the field of recruitment, the quality of elected members may be reduced. There must be many men and women of high ability who would be willing to serve on local authorities but who are unwilling to give unswerving support to a party or who happen to belong to a political minority in their own locality. The other main causes of complaint are that where councillors organise themselves into political groups, decisions are taken by the majority group in private meetings, and that politics are allowed to affect details of local administration which are quite beyond the normal bounds of party controversy.

Equally, however, a strong case can be made in favour of party politics. Party activity does much to increase interest in local elections: party conflict tends to reduce the number of unopposed elections, and to raise the proportion of the electorate who vote in contested elections. Further, if a candidate is returned without a party label, it does not follow that he has no political affiliations but merely that he has not declared any he may have. To argue that politics should be taken out of local government is, in part, to misunderstand the nature of politics. In a democracy we argue freely about the proper aims and methods of public policy. This is political discussion. Inevitably, the major questions which confront local authorities, education, housing, planning, raise issues which are political in nature and attract the attention of political organisations. The idea that these matters should be left to 'the best man for the job' is fanciful since one cannot decide who is the best man unless the opinions of candidates are revealed. The charge that party groups should not have private 'caucus' meetings to settle policy is countered by showing that this is analogous to what happens in our national government; no one suggests it is wrong for Conservative and Labour MPs to hold separate private gatherings or that party leaders should not meet in conditions of secrecy at Cabinet or 'Shadow' Cabinet meetings. Party organisation in a democracy is essential for opinions to be organised into broad streams. The group or party representing the dominant stream of opinion becomes responsible for the conduct of public affairs for a limited time, and may be displaced from power at a subsequent election if it displeases the voters. It follows that where the business of a local authority is conducted on a party basis it is more likely to be planned and consistent than if it depends on unorganised and changing views of individual councillors.

Whatever view one takes of these theoretical considerations, it is vital to recognise that the impact of politics on local government is growing steadily. Even in rural areas, most local elections are now fought on a party basis. What does vary, however, and what is most difficult to determine, is how far party organisation affects the actual working of a local council. The variety of local arrangements is best illustrated by the description of extremes. In some councils, party loyalty matters little; members may be elected on a party basis but, once elected, tend to act as individuals; committee chairmen are chosen irrespective of politics and no group meetings are held. This arrangement is becoming increasingly scarce. At the other extreme, party governs everything important. The majority group meets to determine policy on major issues; it secures a majority on all committees; it nominates the chairmen and vice-chairmen of all committees; the parties require complete obedience from their members, and any councillor who refuses to support a party decision is expelled from the group and will not get party support at the next election. Such extensive party influence is common in urban areas and other authorities dominated by the Labour Party. There are, of course, many authorities which fall in between the patterns defined above, where groups meet irregularly or committee chairmanships are not always distributed on a party basis. And sometimes where party loyalties are strong, the effect of politics is restricted because no group has an overall majority of seats.

Against this background of an uneven degree of party activity, the work of elected members, officers and committees continues. Where the party element is strong the ability of elected members to speak their minds freely in public is curtailed. On major issues the only free discussion may take place in the privacy of the party meeting where party policy is decided, if necessary by a vote. An elected member who finds himself in a minority among party colleagues is required to bow to the necessity of political unity and vote against his opinion at committee and council meetings. Where strict party discipline operates, it follows that the policy adopted need not represent the will of the majority, but only the will of the majority of the majority—which may well be a minority of the whole. Further, the officers will have less influence on the direction of local affairs if party considerations govern policy and major decisions are taken at private meetings which officers do not attend. Even so, the picture must not be exaggerated. However intense party activity may be, a mass of minor matters remain to be settled by committee debate and by consultation between chief officers and committee chairmen.

COUNCILLORS

Representative democracy in local government is secured by the regular election of councillors. There are about 25,000 in England and Wales, excluding the minor authorities, the parish and community councils. What type of people are they? Two official surveys provide information. One was undertaken in 1964 for the Maud Committee on management and the more recent study in 1976 was provided for the Committee on the Remuneration of Councillors. A comparison between the surveys shows that the 1972 Act did not have a major effect on the social characteristics of councillors. In 1964 their average age was 55; in 1976 half of them had ages up to 54. The proportion of women rose significantly from 12% to 17%, but they are still greatly under-represented. The proportion of retired people on councils fell from 20% to 16%. Both surveys showed that certain occupations predominated among council members, notably employers, managers, professional workers and farmers; this tendency is unsurprising since such people are best able to fit in with the times of local authority meetings. The biggest change between 1964 and 1976 relates to education: in 1964, 23% of councillors had gained qualifications resulting from higher education while in 1976 this figure had jumped to 50%. The prospect is that this tendency will continue since younger councillors are more likely to have such qualifications than their more elderly colleagues. In 1976 councillors appear to have had average earnings of £4,400—rather above the figure for the whole population: this information is probably less reliable than the rest of the survey because some councillors failed to state their income. Also in 1976, 76% were owner-occupiers, an increase from the 1964 figure of 66%. The ratio of council house tenants remained unchanged at 16%.

These surveys show that councillors do not form a normal cross-section of society. Equally, their social composition is too mixed for them to constitute anything approaching a distinct elite.

The Maud Committee on Management suggested that persons over 70 should be disqualified from election, but this idea has not been accepted. Already Justices of the Peace must retire from the active list at 75. The analogy is not exact because justices are nominated for life while councillors are subject to re-election. Is age disqualification justified? Certainly, the elderly are less likely to be as vigorous or alert as younger people. On the other hand, should not the electors decide when an individual is unsuitable to represent them? The ability to contest an election successfully is at least some evidence of energy, and many councillors over the age of 70 now give excellent service to local government. Yet younger councillors could give even better service.

The 1972 reorganisation did cause a significant fall in the total number of councillors outside London. The reduction was approximately 11,600. And 4,400 aldermen also disappeared. Rural areas suffered the greatest loss of representatives because here rural districts and small urban authorities were joined together. In the largest towns—the former county boroughs—there was often an increase in councillors because these places now elect members to the county council. Since the councillor/electorate ratio was lowest in large towns and highest in country districts, the reorganisation tended to moderate the disproportion. Even so, the variations are very considerable. A member of the Greater London Council represents about 80,000 people. A member of a large non-metropolitan county represents at least 12,000 people. A district councillor is likely to represent on average about 2,000 people. Areas which have third-tier authorities also enjoy supplementary representation through parish or community councillors. Overall it is still true that representation is strongest, in constitutional terms, where population is relatively sparse.

The reduction in the number of councillors implies that those who remain have even heavier duties. If councillors have heavy responsibilities—should they be paid? The Local Government Act, 1948, entitled members of local authorities to claim for loss of earnings on the basis of a somewhat niggardly scale, but this did not constitute payment. It was compensation rather than remuneration, a compromise that avoided paying a salary. The arguments against changing the tradition of honorary public service in local government were formidable. There was no wide demand that it should be altered. Indeed, the Social Survey report to the Maud Committee showed that both councillors and ex-councillors are generally hostile to the idea: the report also showed that lack of time rather than financial reasons was the main barrier to the recruitment of young, well-educated councillors. Payment introduces a new and unpleasant question of motivation: all council candidates are open to the sneer that they wished to be elected to get easy money. Were this type of attitude to become prevalent, it is probable that many people would be deterred from standing and some present councillors might drop out. Payment also increases the burden on the local rate and is thus unlikely to be popular with ratepayers. There is also a difficult question about how much should be paid. If the sums involved are substantial and designed to attract people of ability, the operation must be costly and there can be no guarantee that people of the requisite calibre will come forward—or that they will be elected. Large payments could well attract the wrong sort of person to council work. On the other hand, if the amounts offered are too small, councils may still be dominated by retired persons or those with inadequate ability and experience.

The case for making payments is far stronger. Unless some financial recompense is available for councillors, many people who must spend the greater part of their time earning a living are perforce unable to offer their services and the field of recruitment will be limited to housewives, retired people, the self-employed and those fortunate enough to have sympathetic employers willing to release them for local government work. Elected representatives naturally spend varying amounts of time on council work; their burden will depend on their personal inclinations, the size of the authority and their status within it. Leading councillors in the larger authorities, including the chairmen of major committees, already devote a great deal of time each week to public service. For some these duties become virtually a full-time occupation. Why should we expect all this effort without significant financial cost to the community? If our councillors are to fairly represent all sections of the community, particularly if we want younger and able councillors, payment must be made.

The 1972 Act permits the Government to fix a maximum daily rate that can be paid to councillors for attending to council business. Sums paid are modest; *pro rata* they are no more than the salary of junior local government officers. The rate of payment is the same for all members but the amounts received by individual councillors vary with the time spent on council business. So while no special payments are made to committee chairmen, the likelihood is that many of them receive more than other councillors. The attendance allowance is taxable and is regarded as a net addition to income. People who serve on local authorities but who are not councillors, i.e. co-opted members of committees, get no attendance payment but may claim a financial loss allowance. Members of a local authority and its committees can claim travelling and subsistence allowances when engaged on council business more than three miles from their homes. Parish and community councillors receive no allowance of any kind for duties within the area covered by their own council. Chairmen and vice-chairmen of both county and district councils can also receive an allowance 'to meet the expenses of his office'. Finally, a local authority can insure its members against death or injury caused by accident while engaged on council business. The Callaghan Government appointed a committee under the chairmanship of Mr Derek Robinson to review the problem. Its Report (Cmnd 7010) published in 1977 found that many councillors did suffer financially from their public service. The Committee felt this should be remedied. Accordingly, it proposed that councillors receive a basic sum of £1,000 which would be taxable, together with travel and subsistence allowances. Further, councillors who could show they suffered financial loss from 'approved duties' should be entitled to receive further sums as compensation, the amount of which would be adjusted in accordance with the marginal tax rate of each individual. Another proposal that councillors who have greater responsibilities, i.e. the chairmen of major committees, should get extra payment, is discussed in the following section. No action has been taken on these suggestions.

There are many qualifications governing candidature at local elections. A councillor must be 21 years of age and a British subject. He must also be on the register of electors for the authority concerned, unless during the twelve months prior to the election he has been resident in the area, or it has been his principal place of work, or he has been the owner or tenant of land or buildings within it. For a parish or community councillor the residence qualification is more flexible: he must have lived within three miles of the area during the preceding year. People who satisfy these conditions may still be disqualified by any one of the following rules. An employee of a local authority cannot be an elected member of it. So a teacher employed by a metropolitan district can serve on the county council: a teacher employed for a county council can serve on his district council. Bankruptcy is a disqualification, so is a surcharge of £500 by the district auditor within five years of the election. Those convicted of corrupt practices at elections are barred as well as those convicted for any offence within the last five years for which the penalty imposed was imprisonment for three months or more without the option of a fine. Further, a councillor who is absent from council meetings for six months will vacate his seat unless the authority approves his reason for absence.

The barrier against local authority staff does limit the availability of prospective councillors. No doubt the disqualification is imposed because it is felt that an employee should not join his employing body, as this would produce a conflict of interest. Clearly, it would be inappropriate for an administrative officer to be elected to the council which it is his duty to advise and assist. Whether the ban should extend to all employees, in particular to manual workers, is a matter for argument. They would have to be prohibited from speaking or voting on any resolution affecting their own remuneration or conditions of service. Subject to this safeguard why should a manual worker not be eligible for election? There does seem an element of hypocrisy in a system which disqualifies a dustman from election to his district council because of some alleged conflict of interest but which does not take similar precautions in relation to estate agents, building contractors and surveyors. However the Redcliffe-Maud Committee on Conduct in Local Government recommended firmly that the present restriction on local authority staff should remain unaltered.

Perhaps the most intractable constitutional problem affecting councillors is the relationship between their public duties and their business interests. The law on this topic is now governed by Section 94 of the Local Government Act, 1972. In essence, the position is that a councillor who has a financial interest in any contract or other matter coming before his authority must disclose his interest and not vote or participate in discussion thereon. Failure to observe this rule renders the defaulter liable to a fine not exceeding £200 for each offence: any such prosecution must be initiated by the Director of Public Prosecutions. The details of the law are complex. Interests of a spouse are included in the ban provided the marriage partners are living together. Membership of a partnership or company is also included. But the disability is removed wherever an interest is so remote that it cannot reasonably be regarded as likely to influence a councillor's conduct. And shareholdings in a company do not disqualify where the nominal amount is below £1,000 or below one-hundredth of the issued share capital of the company, whichever is less. A councillor can make a general statement of his interests in writing to be available for inspection by other councillors; this will obviate the need for a specific declaration of interest on each item that is linked to his business concerns. Another escape route is that the Secretary of State can remove this disability from a council on any particular occasion when he feels the public interest so requires, perhaps because so many councillors would otherwise be disqualified. A district council has a similar power of dispensation in relation to a parish council.

Section 94 is decreasingly relevant to the situation. The original legislation, Section 76 of the Local Government Act, 1933, was designed to ensure that there should be no improper influence exercised by businessmen who might have contracts with their local authority. Today the threat to probity in local government is quite different. It is that elected members may use 'inside' information about probable future policy in relation to land use for their private advantage. If a member knows that his authority is likely to take certain action which will affect property values, he may make shrewd bargains before the intentions of the authority reach the stage of formal decisions and become public knowledge. Such behaviour is beyond the scope of Section 94. The problem is not that abuse is widespread but rather the virtual impossibility of formulating legislation that would effectively prevent it. To extend to local government some form of Official Secrets Act is at present beyond the bounds of possibility: it would certainly discourage recruitment of councillors. Many authorities have a Standing Order which decrees that committee business shall be treated as confidential until it is communicated to the council or the press, but such an instruction cannot be a water-tight safeguard against abuse. A council could decide to exclude from its planning committee any member with interests in business or property; the individual application of such a rule could be very unpleasant, it would deprive the planning committee of useful experience and would not necessarily stop the circulation of valuable information. The best safeguards seem to be the consciences of elected members and the pressure of public opinion.

Growing concern about the possible extent of corruption in local government, especially after the various cases connected with the architect John Poulson, led to the appointment of a committee to inquire into standards of conduct in local government. The chairman was Lord Redcliffe-Maud. The Report, published in 1974, concluded that local government was essentially honest but that corruption spreads unless it is stopped. So a number of additional precautions were proposed. The Committee recommended that the law on disclosure of interests be made tougher. Councillors should be required to disclose an interest orally and thereafter withdraw from the meeting while the relevant item was under discussion unless a dispensation had been received from the Secretary of State. Councillors should also be required to enter certain interests on a public register. A councillor should not be chairman of a committee whose affairs are linked to his personal interests; sometimes councillors should not even be members. The use of information received through membership of a local authority for private gain should be a criminal offence. The report argued that 'openness' in local administration was a valuable safeguard. It also recommended that the associations of local authorities draw up a national code of conduct for all councillors; this would define standards and have an important persuasive force.

The discussion of pecuniary interests raises the question of motive. Why do people continue to serve for long periods on local authorities? No authoritative answer to this question is possible. If elected members are asked why they serve, their replies will be highly subjective. Obviously they may be fired by political enthusiasm or be attracted by whatever prestige is associated with the word 'councillor'. It is probably true that most elected members feel that they are doing something useful for the community. A council and its committees become a sort of informal club which the retired members, in particular, find attractive. It is also possible that a few people join local councils out of the hope that financial advantage will be derived therefrom: certainly this is sometimes believed to be so by the general public. Should the idea spread that councillors are in local government for what they can get out of it, persons jealous of their reputation will avoid membership of local authorities. The 'club' would cease to be an attractive one. Here the problem is put bluntly, not because of any immediate prospect that this situation will occur but because it is a danger not to be overlooked. The maintenance of probity in local government is of the utmost importance from every point of view.

LEADERS, CHAIRMEN AND MAYORS

In theory, all councillors have equal status and an equal right to influence the business of their local authority. In practice, councillors are by no means equal to each other. Party groups elect leaders. The Leader of the majority group is often known as the leader of the council—in effect a local Prime Minister. He (or she) may achieve a position of dominance. Chairmen of major committees can attain a key role in the work of a particular department of a local authority. Councillors who have not been chosen for such positions, in parliamentary terms the backbenchers, necessarily have much less influence. A variety of factors help the ruling elite to keep their place. They are usually more experienced than their critics; they spend more time on council business and are better informed; above all, they draw support from the conventions imposed by party loyalty. Where a council is run on strict party lines, backbenchers will not be expected to challenge their own party's policy at formal council and committee meetings. Dissent has to be restricted to private party meetings. Here a determined chairman may be able to ride roughshod over any opponents, especially as the time available for these meetings may be short. There have been some behind-the-scenes rows about how far detailed information should be made available to backbench members of a majority group. They may be told that if they demand information, it must be made available equally to their political opponents, the councillors in the minority group(s). If the material is damaging then it will be used to harass the majority and can even have repercussions at local elections. So where party machines are tightly organised, a backbench councillor can feel as far away from the seats of power as a backbench MP. There is no doubt that opportunities for local corruption have been facilitated by authoritarian party structures which have helped the malefactors to evade criticism and detection.

Of course, the concept of the 'city boss' is not entirely new. Joseph Chamberlain was a dominant figure in Birmingham in the 1870s. In the early years of this century Alderman Salvidge had enormous sway in Liverpool as did Sir Sidney Kimber in Southampton. But these men depended on personality rather than strict party discipline.

The question of payments for councillors, discussed in the previous section, becomes even more acute in the case of those exercising leadership. These people will be spending more time on council work. Many will also be involved in the activities of the associations of local authorities. At this stage local government becomes virtually a full-time occupation. A large majority of those who have to earn a living could not adjust to a schedule of this kind without severe financial loss. How can this problem be solved? Should those who have exceptional responsibilities receive exceptional payment?

The Robinson Committee felt it was essential that extra pay should be available. It recommended that up to one-tenth of the councillors on a local authority, subject to a maximum of eight, should get more money. So the special responsibilities of the Leader, the Mayor or Chairman and up to 'six committee chairmen could be recognised. The amount paid should depend on the size of the authority: the smallest authorities below 50,000 population should pay an extra £750, on top of the £1,000 that would go to all councillors, while at the other extreme where population exceeded 400,000, the extra pay should be £3,000. The Robinson Report appeared in 1977 so today the sums paid would have to be much higher to provide the real return envisaged in the Report.

The Local Government Bill 1979 authorises extra payments for councillors with special responsibilities. Various problems may arise. Should a minority group Leader benefit? Elections for Leader and committee chairmen may arouse greater tensions and jealousies than in the past. Will the public understand that not all councillors get the extra pay? The backbench councillor may be irked by his lack of influence; he will be even more irritated if he finds that he is generally believed to be getting a considerable salary. And anyone who stands for election, especially to a large authority, might be open to the charge of seeking to make money from political and public service.

The first business at the annual meeting of a local authority is to elect the chairman. A chairman may be the most influential member of his council, keeping in regular touch with senior officials about policy developments and giving general direction to affairs. Alternatively, at least during his year of office, he may stand aside from controversial matters and perceive his main duty to be the impartial control of council meetings. Where party organisation is strong the latter model is likely to be adopted. Local traditions depend upon the political situation. The method of filling the office is a good guide to how it is used. If a new chairman is elected each year, possibly on the basis of seniority or as a result of agreement between political groups, then he is likely to exercise minimum influence. But if a chairman is re-elected time and time again, one suspects that he is an important force in council affairs.

The essential difference between a Mayor and a chairman is that the latter does not have such an intense social programme. District and county chairmen will make some appearances on public occasions and may wear a chain of office, but their status is not so high. Yet a Mayor has dignity rather than power. In some other countries the title 'Mayor' describes an official who has substantial personal responsibilities for the proper conduct of local administration. The French *maire* is in this position. In the United States the situation is complicated because there are many forms of town government and the traditional Mayor and council pattern has often been replaced by other systems thought to be more efficient or to provide firmer safeguards against corruption, but where the Mayor survives he generally has substantial personal responsibilities, analogous to those of the President in relation to the federal government. The British Mayor has a quite different position. His executive tasks are minimal. His main formal duty is to preside at council meetings and ensure that these are conducted properly in accordance with the rules of council procedure. But Mayors are always busy people. They are expected to undertake a formidable programme of appearances at various public occasions, to entertain distinguished visitors who come to their borough, to attend civic, cultural and charitable events, school speechdays and to visit local hospitals, especially on Christmas Day. This whirl of social activity is punctuated by speeches of welcome and votes of thanks. The Mayor becomes the embodiment of the community of the borough. By statute he has precedence over all other persons save a direct representative of the Crown such as the Lord-Lieutenant of the county. The Mayoralty is held in deep respect, but the respect belongs to the office and not to the man who holds it. This respect demands that the Mayor abstain from controversial activities—in the same way as the Speaker of the House of Commons: the general pattern is that the Mayor takes no part in political events during his period of office. It follows that he does not concern himself with the details of local administration. He does not direct or supervise borough officers. If important decisions have to be taken between committee meetings, the responsibility falls on the appropriate committee chairman rather than the Mayor. The normal position is that the Mayor will exercise initiative only in unusual circumstances and then in a non-controversial manner. Thus if there is a local disaster the Mayor may open a relief fund; by acting in this way he is not so much providing leadership as expressing the conscience of the community. The Mayoralty, then, is of much civic significance but does not bestow great influence over local affairs.

OFFICERS

The term 'local government officer' creates a mind-picture of people who work at desks in the local town hall or county hall. In fact,

office-workers form but a fraction of the total employees of local
authorities. Not only do local councils need the services of a large
'outdoor' manual staff concerned largely with cleansing operations
and construction work, but a wide variety of skills are also required,
e.g. teachers, policemen, welfare workers, if all local government
duties are to be carried out effectively. But the administrative and
clerical staff in the local offices are at the heart of the administrative
system and for this reason demand our special attention.

The days when the parish, as the most important unit of local
government, could rely on the services of part-time unpaid officers
are long past. Elected members have neither the time nor the range
of professional expertise necessary to direct all the business of a
local authority. Parliament therefore insisted that certain officers be
appointed. Each county, borough and district had to have a clerk,
treasurer and medical officer of health; all, except a rural district,
had to have a surveyor; all, except a county, had to have a public
health inspector. These legal provisions have historical significance
in that they recall some unwillingness in the nineteenth century to
make certain appointments, notably in relation to health. They also
helped to create a uniformity in the pattern of local authority
departments. Today there are fewer specific requirements in relation
to the appointment of staff. The provisions mentioned above have
all been swept away. However, the 1972 Act retained ten categories
of officials whose employment by local authorities is compulsory:
they are police officers, members of fire brigades, chief education
officers, directors of social services, public analysts, agricultural
analysts, weights and measures inspectors, accountants to inspect
the books of pools promoters, accountants and 'experienced mechani-
cians' to supervise totalisator operations and the Greater London
Council must appoint district surveyors. The first four items in this
list are the most significant because they imply that local authorities
responsible for police, fire brigades, education and social services
must organise them in separate departments.

Local authorities appoint a Chief Executive with overall responsibility for the efficiency of the whole organisation. No specific
qualifications are required for this post. Yet the choices made by the
new councils in 1973 were very conservative; nearly always a Clerk
or Deputy Clerk was chosen. A few Treasurers were appointed and
Birmingham selected a Chief Planning Officer. Somerset was more
adventurous and appointed a Chief Executive from outside the local
government field; the sequel is mentioned below. A Chief Executive
is in a strong position to exert influence. He is expected to co-ordinate
the work of the separate departments and through the Management
Team is kept in touch with all major issues of policy. Yet much

depends on the personality of the individual. If he is respected because of his ability and other personal qualities, he will be consulted willingly by other chief officers and possibly by committee chairmen. If he is disliked or feared, his influence may be less and certainly will be achieved less happily. The most successful top administrators recognise that their main duty is to interpret the mind of their local authority rather than to mould it.

According to the Local Government Act 1972 a local authority appoints staff 'on such reasonable terms and conditions, including conditions as to remuneration' as the authority sees fit. In fact, conditions of employment are negotiated through Whitley Councils consisting of representatives of employers and employees. Often government policy has an important influence on these negotiations, particularly in regard to teachers' salaries. Officers are protected from arbitrary dismissal both by their conditions of service and by the strength of trade unionism in local government. Policemen have additional safeguards. A chief constable cannot be dismissed without Home Office consent. Any policeman who is dismissed or required to resign can appeal to the Home Secretary. One other safeguard was repealed by the Local Government Act 1972—the stipulation that the Clerk of a county council could be dismissed only with ministerial consent. In 1974 the Somerset County Council proceeded to dismiss their Chief Executive who had held office for only a few months. This incident caused great concern to SOLACE, the Society of Local Authorities' Chief Executives, which felt that some type of appeal or conciliation machinery should be established to deal with any future similar cases. However, a council cannot be expected to retain the services of a chief officer if it has no faith in his judgement or personal suitability to hold a post of great responsibility. The way out of these difficulties is to pay compensation for loss of office.

Ministerial control over appointments is also used in a few cases to prevent the selection of anyone felt to be unsuitable. The Home Secretary must approve the nomination of chief constables; there have been cases where this approval has been withheld because it was proposed to fill a vacancy by internal promotion within the local force. Similarly, he must approve the appointment of chief fire officers. The DHSS has to approve the qualifications of Directors of Social Services. Whether controls of this nature are necessary or desirable is a matter of controversy. If a local authority is regarded by Parliament as being fully capable of choosing a Chief Executive or Treasurer—why is it not capable of choosing a chief fire officer?

There has been some reduction in central controls over local staff selection. No longer does the Secretary of State have to approve the appointment of a chief education officer. No longer do firemen have to be British subjects or citizens of the Republic of Ireland. But the minimum chest measurements of firemen are still prescribed by statutory instrument. The major safeguard against bad appointments is the requirement that officers in positions of responsibility should have appropriate professional qualifications. Sometimes this stipulation has a statutory basis, otherwise it is conventional or included in the schedule of agreements made through the Whitley machinery governing pay and conditions of service for local government officers. This demand for professional qualifications has certain effects on the recruitment of staff which are discussed in Chapter VII, but they are valuable in that they ensure a minimum quality of proficiency and obviate much of the possibility of corruption in making appointments. Another feature of the local government service is that promotion is obtained through moving from place to place, gaining wider experience of different conditions.

Officers of a local authority must now declare their interest in any contract involving their authority. The principle is the same as that applied to councillors. The declaration is to be in writing. Conscious failure to observe this rule renders the offender liable to a fine not exceeding £200. Whereas the prosecution of a councillor for this type of offence must be undertaken by the Director of Public Prosecutions, no such limitation is placed upon the prosecution of an official. The Redcliffe-Maud Committee on Conduct in Local Government recommended that officers should make oral disclosures of interests at meetings in the same way as councillors. It also proposed that a register of officers interests be kept which would be open to inspection by councillors. Further, senior and professional staff should be required to agree not to take up other employment in their authority's area, without the authority's consent, for a period of two years after leaving local government service.

The central issue which affects senior local government officers is the nature of their relationship with their employing authority—how far can officers persuade elected members to accede to their views? In law, there is no problem. A council decides policy and instructs its officers to carry out its wishes; officers, as servants of the council, must obey. However, in conformity with the general law of master and servant, a local government officer cannot escape the consequences of an illegal act by pleading that he was acting under the instructions of his council. In a notable application of this principle the courts have held (*Attorney General* v. *De Winton*, 1906) that a Borough Treasurer must disobey an order from his Council that calls for an illegal payment: the argument here is that a Borough Treasurer is not a mere servant of his council but has a fiduciary responsibility to the burgesses as a whole. If a Treasurer refused to carry out an instruction from his council because of doubts about its legality, it would still be open to the council, at least in theory, to dismiss their Treasurer. If ever a dispute threatened to reach this stage, public opinion would be aroused and play a large part in deciding the issue. There is no parallel ruling governing the position of a Clerk if faced with what he feels to be an illegal instruction. All that can be said is that if a Clerk wishes to secure his position against possible action by the District Auditor, he must at least ensure that the dubious instruction is given by the council as a whole and not merely by an influential member or group of members (*Re Hurle-Hobbs ex parte Riley and another*, 1944).

The inferior status of officers is symbolised by some authorities through the seating arrangements in their council chamber, for the Chief Executive sits immediately below the dais where the chairman (or Mayor) presides over council meetings. This layout is extremely inconvenient whenever the chairman wishes to consult the Chief Executive. Elsewhere the Chief Executive is permitted to sit on the left hand side of the Chair; this makes it easy, perhaps too easy, for the Chief Executive to offer advice. Most officials are unhappy about proffering advice at a public council meeting except on matters of procedure where the need may be simply to remind the council of its own standing orders. They prefer to advise in the privacy of committee meetings. Necessarily the officers have a store of information which elected members would be foolish to ignore. Officers can draw upon a lifetime of professional experience and will know, or should know, not merely the legal, financial and technical complications of matters that come before committees, but the various ministerial rulings and advice as set out in Departmental Circulars and other official publications. Obviously, an official may present factual information in such a way as to lead elected members towards the policy he thinks best. But advice must always be presented tactfully. A committee resents an official who appears overbearing or impatient. A wise officer knows that a committee should always feel that it has itself made the decisions. The influence of officers tends to be greatest where an authority meets least frequently and where it is not tightly controlled by a political group: these conditions apply in some county councils. Officers view the advent of party politics in local government with mixed feelings. On the one hand, it reduces the impact they can make on policy; on the other, it probably assists continuity and certainty of policy, for once the dominant group has decided upon a course of action it is loath to retract. The party element also strengthens the need for local government officers, like civil servants, to be non-political. Where one party has controlled an authority for many years there is a danger that chief officers will be identified with the ruling party—a situation that can cause great difficulty should the party control change hands. It follows that aspiring politicians should not seek to become local administrators. Local government employees, other than teachers, rarely gain political prominence.

STANDING ORDERS

Methods of procedure in local government are necessarily more complex, some would say clumsy, than the administrative processes in industry or commerce. Since local authorities spend public money they have a special duty to see that it is properly spent: risks which are commonly taken by private enterprise are less acceptable in public administration. The other difference is that local councils reach decisions after discussion, much of which is held in public, because in a democracy the public have a right to know how public business is being conducted. So to ensure that their affairs are conducted in a regular and orderly manner, local authorities draw up Standing Orders to regulate their own conduct. These are in addition to the statutory controls in the law of local government and they must not, of course, transgress statutory provisions.

Standing Orders are mainly concerned with laying down rules of debate and with the procedure for using the council seal and for dealing with tenders and contracts. The form of Standing Orders varies very much between authorities so that no detailed description would have general application. However, they will always govern the order of business at council meetings and how various types of motion or amendments may be moved. Some councils impose a time limit on speeches. This raises a number of issues: how much time should each member be given; how much preferential treatment, if any, should be given to the chairman of a committee or the mover of a motion; how far should there be a right of reply? It is much better to avoid any time limits, but this may not be possible in large authorities or where debates are animated by political differences. The major item of business at a normal council meeting is the consideration of minutes or reports from committees. Again, this can be organised in various ways. Committee chairmen may present their minutes or reports in turn and any questions or arguments about committee proposals may be allowed when the council is asked to approve them paragraph by paragraph. The danger of this method is that the council may spend an excessive amount of time on the affairs of those committees which happen to come early on the agenda. To try to obviate this imbalance of attention, Standing Orders may lay down an alternative procedure. This often takes the form of requiring the Clerk to read through the numbers of the paragraphs of each committee report: a member may interrupt to ask a committee chairman a question on the contents of a paragraph, but if he wishes to start an argument and challenge policy, he will say simply 'Object'. Then when the Clerk has finished reading through the paragraph numbers, the council proceeds to discuss the items to which objection has been taken. In this way members can get a conspectus of the total amount of contentious business before them and this may help them to use debating time more sparingly and effectively. Standing Orders can also guard against another danger—that a council will be rushed into hasty decisions without adequate prior consideration. There is a statutory rule that a county or district council cannot consider any business unless it has been specified in a notice summoning the meeting sent out three days in advance. This rule may be modified by local Standing Orders which may also extend the principle to committees. They also contain provisions to support the authority of the Chair in moments of disorder, may provide for the reception of petitions and deputations, and govern relationships between a council and its committees.

A main concern of Standing Orders is to maintain probity in local administration. They may incorporate rules about the declaration of interests by both councillors and officials. They will prescribe how tenders shall be invited and the form of submission. A general instruction is that the amount of a tender shall be treated as confidential in order to secure genuine competition among contractors. Conditions may be laid down to require compliance with specifications issued by the British Standards Institution. There is some feeling that Standing Orders may be unduly restrictive and inhibit the development of efficient purchasing procedures. They also define the extent and the circumstances under which the authority's powers may be delegated.

Standing Orders are a vital element in the constitution of a local authority. They help to ensure harmonious operation and financial regularity. It is, of course, essential that they are understood both by elected members and by officers in positions of responsibility. Officers must observe the detailed regulations covering contracts and financial management; elected members will not be able to play a full part in discussion unless they know when and how they may intervene.

Chapter VII

THE QUEST FOR EFFICIENCY

The development of ideas on the best way to organise the business of local authorities has been greatly stimulated by three official reports. In 1964 the Minister of Housing and Local Government appointed two committees of enquiry at the request of the main associations of local authorities. One Committee, with Sir George Mallaby as chairman, was required to investigate the staffing of local government. The other had wider terms of reference: 'to consider in the light of modern conditions how local government might best continue to attract and retain people (both elected representatives and principal officers) of the calibre necessary to ensure its maximum effectiveness'. Under the guidance of its chairman Sir John Maud (now Lord Redcliffe-Maud) this Committee undertook a far-reaching investigation into the management of local authorities. Both Committees reported in 1967 and these important documents will be discussed more fully below. The mere fact that these two enquiries were set in motion did indicate a widespread malaise about local government: indeed, the terms of reference clearly imply concern about the quality of the people in local government. No great institution can be efficient if those who work for it have limited ability or poor morale and if the public 'image' of the institution deters other more suitable persons from coming forward to help with the work. The Maud Committee proposed fundamental reforms in the internal organisation of local authorities because it felt that if councillors and officials were frustrated by petty and time-wasting methods of doing business, then able people would be less willing to concern themselves with the management of local public affairs.

The third report came from a Committee set up in 1971 as a joint venture by the DOE and the four local authority associations to advise upon management arrangements for the new authorities to be created in the major reform of structure then in prospect. A steering committee was formed under the chairmanship of Sir Frank Marshall and consisted largely of representatives of the associations: the detailed recommendations were produced by a working group headed by Mr Bains, Clerk of the Kent County Council. This latter body, with a single exception, was made up of senior local government officers. The document they produced will be referred to below as the Bains Report. But the main difference between the Bains Committee and the earlier Maud and Mallaby enquiries was that it had an immediate and precise task—to try and discover how the imminent changes could be made to work to the best advantage. Maud and Mallaby, operating with a more flexible time-scale, had to try to educate local government opinion on the need for change in the traditional *modus operandi*.

Apart from new ideas on management and establishment work, local administration has been greatly affected by the onward march of technology. Sophisticated equipment replaces men and women. Much routine office work is taken over by computers. The staff are called upon to learn fresh skills. New concepts in accountancy and new applications of mathematics are used to produce material which forms a better base for making decisions. This chapter outlines the various approaches to the task of making local government more efficient.

PERSONNEL MANAGEMENT

The officers of local authorities do not constitute a single body, such as the Civil Service, employed by one master. Each authority determines its own establishment of staff and appoints its own officials. Except in the few instances where appointment or dismissal is subject to ministerial consent, and in the few cases in which there is some central prescription of qualifications, each authority is free to recruit its own officers in its own way, and to impose what qualifications it desires. Nevertheless, the whole body of local government officers possesses many uniform characteristics and in recent years has conformed increasingly to standards and uniformities introduced into pay, service conditions, entry and promotion tests, and other elements in the officer's contract of service with his employing authority. These developments are due, partly to trade union organisation among the staffs themselves, and partly to joint organisation of both the staffs and the local authorities in Whitley machinery for collective bargaining. The local government officers trade union NALGO persuaded Parliament to pass legislation in 1937 to establish a unified superannuation scheme for local government. This facilitated the movement of officers between authorities, opened up better promotion prospects and enabled officers to acquire a wider range of experience. In the inter-war period NALGO also struggled hard to establish Whitley machinery, i.e. to create joint consultation with employers over questions of pay and conditions of service. While such consultation was operative in some areas, it was not until 1944 that a National Joint Council was established with the agreement of the associations of local authorities. The National Joint Council is supplemented by Provincial Councils which deal with local problems. In 1946 the NJC approved a national scheme of salaries and service conditions, known as 'the charter', providing a framework of scales for the grading of posts. This is now operative throughout the country and it has been supplemented by agreements for standard gradings among certain classes of officer. Other negotiating committees have agreed upon scales of pay and standard conditions of service for the Chief Officers of local authorities.

The Whitley machinery also became responsible for settling standards of recruitment, training and qualification. It enlisted the help of university staff, the governing bodies of the professions and the various occupational groups of the service in deciding the standards to be enforced. This policy was implemented by the NJC through the establishment, under its auspices, of a Local Government Examinations Board. This Board had advisory functions on questions of education, qualifications and training and also organised examinations, the syllabuses for which concentrated on government and administration. Success at these examinations (or in obtaining equivalent qualifications offered by professional bodies) became a prerequisite, but not a guarantee, of advancing beyond certain grades in the local government hierarchy. Local government is now open to the criticism that it is examination ridden. Yet this emphasis on paper qualifications has ensured a high level of professional competence among officials. It has also done much to eliminate canvassing or corruption in the making of local appointments.

These arrangements for recruitment and training worked tolerably well until the nineteen-sixties presented local authorities with a fresh kind of staffing problem—their ability to attract and retain staff of adequate calibre. In earlier years this had presented no difficulty. Boys from the grammar schools had been keen to enter local government because it offered both security and prospects of promotion to positions of respect in society. After entry, young men studied for various professional examinations and obtained promotion by moving round from one authority to another, and in due course the most able of them became chief officials. (Directors of Education were exceptions to this pattern as they are required to have university training.) Thus the local authorities had no worries about the quality of their staff as the grammar schools provided a steady flow of excellent recruits. Now this source of supply is less fruitful since an increasing proportion of young people with good GCE results leave school to follow various kinds of further education—at universities, colleges of technology, teacher training colleges, etc. Few are left for local government. This problem faced other professions that have traditionally recruited school-leavers. But local authorities did appear to be in greater difficulty, perhaps because their 'image' seems dull and uninspiring. This is not to assert that local government is dull and uninspiring. Like beauty, the image of local government is in the eye of the beholder.

Essentially this is the situation that faced the Mallaby Committee. Its central recommendations were predictable. Local authorities should improve their liaison arrangements with schools to show school-leavers that local administration offers an attractive and worthwhile career. Also they must recruit more university graduates and make the best possible use of the abilities of their staff. So the Mallaby Committee proposed various developments in post-entry training for staff, ranging from induction training for junior entrants to management training for senior staff. At the local level the Clerk of the authority should have an overall responsibility for establish-ment work including training; at the national level the Committee proposed the creation of a Local Government Training Board which should both exercise some general supervision over the nature of training and also provide a central organisation which would enable local authorities to pool the cost. The smaller, poorer authorities, and those in remote areas, found it difficult or impossible to provide adequate facilities for young officers who wished to obtain qualifica-tions; such authorities could not recruit ambitious young people. To pool the cost of training on a national basis would help the poorer authorities and thus ease the problem. The associations of local authorities accepted this recommendation immediately. The Local Government Training Board was established in 1968 and also incorporated the work of the Local Government Examinations Board.

One of the Mallaby recommendations was undeniably contro-versial—that local authorities should provide a career structure for lay administrative officers which would take them up to the second or third tier position in a local authority department. The use of the term 'lay administrative officer' is curious and potentially mis-leading; in normal usage, a 'lay' member of a local authority is thought to be an elected representative. The Mallaby Committee thought of a 'lay' officer as one who had not obtained a specialised professional qualification but who, instead, had obtained a broad education at a university or had studied for the LGEB qualifica-tion, the Diploma in Municipal Administration. There is a clear analogy here with the general administrators who occupy the most senior posts in the Civil Service. The 1972 Bains Report took a different view. It asserted that local government could obtain staff through the professions who would provide the necessary leadership in management. Yet this Report also recognised the value of wider horizons by suggesting that able young officers be encouraged to make 'horizontal' moves from one department to another within an authority. This could mean a move into a post where an officer's qualifications were not immediately relevant to his work. The idea is attractive but it presents obvious difficulties.

These conflicting proposals raise the long-standing argument over the value of general education as opposed to specialised qualifications. Does a training confined to law, accountancy, engineering or medicine narrow the mind and so render men less able to carry out managerial functions? Is the man lacking specialised knowledge so much in the hands of specialists when dealing with practical problems as to be unable to provide effective leadership? The arguments are familiar. However, it is too often overlooked that the ability to administer, to make people work together as a team, to know when to use initiative and when to be cautious, to carry responsibility squarely but not too heavily—all these are functions of aptitude and personality, the development of which is perhaps but slightly affected by the subjects a person studies. If our senior Civil Servants are excellent administrators, is this because of the nature of their academic studies at Oxbridge or because they gained great benefit from the Oxbridge environment in their formative years?

The Mallaby Report did not have any great effect on the recruitment and promotion policies of local authorities. Indeed, the tendency has been to develop management services rather than personnel services. No doubt this is because management services appear to make a direct contribution to efficiency and cost reduction while career development policies increase expenditure and the benefits are not so immediate or so obvious. The Bains Committee urged that the status of personnel work in local government should be raised; that it should be kept separate from the development of management services with co-ordination exercised at a high level; that the word 'establishment' be dropped in favour of 'personnel management'.

The Local Government Training Board adjusted its regulations for the Diploma in Municipal Administration in 1972 in response to the Mallaby view that the status of the general administrator in local government should be enhanced. The intention is that the DMA shall more closely equal the final examinations of other professional bodies so that the career prospects of those who hold the DMA are improved. Whether the tactic will succeed is doubtful. No official figures are available but it is certain that an increasing flow of graduates is entering local government and that most of the graduates hold qualifications related to the various specialised professions that serve local government. There seems no reason why these people should not fill all, or virtually all, the more senior posts in the local government service since the various professional associations are becoming more concerned about post-qualification training, especially in the fields of administration and management. The new generation of specialised graduate entrants will thus be better equipped to undertake higher administrative duties. In these circumstances the outlook for the lay administrative officer is not bright.

The 1974 remapping of areas cannot fail to have some impact on the prospects of local government officers. Fewer authorities with larger departments must reduce the chances of an individual reaching the level of chief officer or a deputy. Again, if there are fewer separate employers, the opportunities to move from one authority to another must be diminished. If departments are larger there may be a greater tendency for middle-ranking posts to be filled by internal promotion. And as authorities become more uniform in size the possibilities for a knight's move type of promotion will disappear: no longer can the Town Clerk of a smaller borough become Deputy Town Clerk of a much larger county borough. The barriers between the two tiers of councils may become even more difficult to traverse, with county officials remaining with counties and district officials with districts. Further, this does involve divisions within a profession, e.g. district planners being separate from county planners. A tendency to split local government officers into competing cadres depending on the status of their employers existed before the reorganisation. The pity is that this situation is likely to be aggravated. Perhaps the most important long-term effect of reorganisation on staffing was to encourage the early retirement of a large number of chief officers and their deputies. A greater number of senior posts are now held by relatively young men so for the next decade the number of vacancies at the top of the tree will be relatively low. Able and ambitious officers at third- and fourth-tier rank are likely to experience growing frustration as the years go by.

To turn to the national level, no action has been taken to institute a Central Staffing Organisation as recommended by the Mallaby Committee. However, the Consultative Council on Local Government Finance is fully conscious of the need to promote the efficient use of staff and the local authority associations are alert to the manpower implications of the development of services. Meanwhile there are three national bodies concerned in various ways with local government staff—the LGTB (Local Government Training Board), LACSAB (Local Authorities Conditions of Service Advisory Board) and LAMSAC (Local Authorities Management Services Advisory Committee). There would be a simplification of machinery if these bodies could be united into one. Yet there are great obstacles in the way. In particular, the unions have a different role in each of these organisations. They nominate members to LGTB; they negotiate with LACSAB; they are held at arm's length by LAMSAC. And as long as local authorities jealously maintain the status of independent and individual employers it will be impossible to move far with the development of national personnel policies.

Training is essentially the responsibility of each local authority. It covers, or should cover, all classes of employee—not only clerical and administrative staff. The role of the Local Government Training Board is to identify and assess training needs, advise councils on how best these needs can be met, and provide a service to support the efforts of the local authorities. Where necessary, the Board produces training material, arranges courses and offers a limited advisory service. Acting with educational institutions, the Board also organises courses in areas such as management education, whereby valuable resources at both universities and polytechnics are developed to meet the special needs of local government; this work also has an experimental aspect in that new courses can be developed for future provision on a wider scale. It also mounts a research programme aimed primarily at developing training methods and material and evaluating the training provided. Originally the Board was financed by a voluntary levy paid by local authorities and, in return, the Board made grants to help local authorities to pay for their training programmes. However, this system ran into difficulties. Some councillors questioned whether the benefit was worth the cost. Some smaller authorities never joined the scheme at all. So the levy/grant principle was ended. Now the Board is financed by receiving a sum from the Rate Support Grant and the amount of this allocation is agreed by the associations of local authorities. The Board is still able to provide a limited financial incentive by way of grants to local authorities to stimulate new types of training; at the present time these 'pump-priming' arrangements are used to stimulate instruction programmes for manual workers and the local training officers themselves.

CO-ORDINATION OF POLICY AND ADMINISTRATION

The final section of Chapter III explained the crying need for co-ordination within the framework of a local authority. How is it to be achieved? The traditional answer has been through the Clerk of the council. A succession of official reports urged this solution in varying terms. The Royal Commission on Local Government recommended in 1929 that the Clerk was the most suitable officer to achieve co-ordination and suggested that his ability to perform this task would depend on his personality. It did not propose that the Clerk be put in a position to give instructions to other chief officers. In 1934 the Hadow Committee on the Recruitment, Training and Promotion of Local Government Officers thought that the essential qualification of a Clerk was administrative ability. This view naturally opens up the argument whether a Clerk should necessarily have legal qualifications. The Treasury O and M Report on Coventry in 1953 again laid heavy emphasis on the administrative role of the Clerk; he should give continual consideration to measures which would achieve economies and be responsible for establishment work and an organisation and methods service. This type of recommendation involves a very real difficulty. If the Clerk is to have an overall responsibility for the effective operation of all his council's activities, then he must be put in a position of seniority over other chief officers so that he is able, when necessary, to insist that they accept measures he feels requisite to improve efficiency. Naturally this involves some down-grading, some loss of independence, by other heads of departments and some change in the traditional practice that a chief officer is responsible to the council through his committee. Without some loss of departmental independence there can be no guarantee that a local authority's administration is an effective unity.

The Maud Report on *Management of Local Government*, leaning on the experience of foreign countries and of experiments at home at Newcastle and elsewhere, stressed more firmly than earlier official reports that the Clerk should be the undisputed head of the council's staff. Since the legal profession is not a unique source of leadership ability and managerial acumen, it accepted also that the Clerk need not be a lawyer.

The Committee produced a comprehensive plan to ensure co-ordination of both administration and policy in local authorities, which involved a drastic reappraisal of the nature of committee work and the structure of local administration. A diagram illustrating the essence of the Maud proposals is given above. The core of this scheme was that each council should appoint a 'management board' consisting of between five and nine members of the council. The management board would formulate major policies and present them for approval to the council; it would have overall responsibility for the execution of these policies; it would take decisions on matters which exceeded the authority of chief officers; it would recommend proposals to the council on items which exceeded its own delegated powers. The Clerk would be responsible to the management board and through it to the council; he would also be the undisputed head of the whole of the staff. The heads of departments would be answerable to the Clerk and *not* to any committee. Obviously this plan provides unity and centralisation of decision-making achieved by down-grading all principal officers other than the Clerk and by down-grading all committees in relation to the management board. Thus in the diagram the unbroken lines indicate chains of command and the broken lines are channels of advice. The Maud Committee was specific about the new role of committees: 'Committees should not be directing or controlling bodies nor should they be concerned with routine administration.' What then are the committees to do? They would make recommendations to the management board on 'major objectives' and study how these could best be carried out. They would review progress in the sphere of the particular service that concerned them, consider reactions of the public and deal with any matters referred to them by the management board. Executive decisions would only be made in exceptional circumstances and when the management board required this to be done; the implication is that delegated authority would normally be given to officers rather than committees. The scheme also permitted a committee to consider any matter raised by its own members, but this seems to conflict with the principle noted above that committees would not consider routine administration.

The general effect would have been to transform each local government unit into a minor model of our system of national government. The council was Parliament, or perhaps the House of Commons; the management board was the Cabinet; the committees were to be analogous to the new specialist committees recently established in the Commons to exercise a general advisory function in a particular field. Just as the Commons is composed largely of backbenchers with a lesser number of Government Ministers, so local authorities would have two classes of members, those on the management board and the rank-and-file committee members.

Service on the management board would inevitably consume much time, so the Maud Committee proposed that its members receive part-time salaries. They urged that emphasis be placed on the collective responsibility of the management board in the same way, presumably, as we think of the collective responsibility of the Cabinet. To quote the Maud Report again, 'Individual members of the management board should have special spheres of interest and speak on them': this appears to mean that one member would become the local Chancellor of the Exchequer, another the local Minister of Education, another the local Minister of Transport and so on. Committee meetings would normally be open to the press: meetings of the management board would be private: most committee meetings in the Commons are public, but Cabinet meetings are not! The parallels are remarkably close.

Inevitably this Report aroused much criticism, a lot of which was defensive and came from those who wished to retain established positions. And before reviewing the objections one should also stress that they are themselves a tribute to the quality of the Report. If a scheme contains little that is new, if its proposals can easily be condemned, then it merits a minimum of attention. Because the Maud Report raised fundamental issues about our local government institutions and illuminated serious shortcomings in their practical operation, it stimulated a great debate.

To force local government to move towards our system of national government is to introduce the deficiencies of Parliament into local government. Thus MPs have insufficient information to act as a check on government departments. Under the Maud plan would councillors have enough information to be able to challenge the management board? The Maud scheme called for fewer committees and a maximum committee membership of 15 to include co-opted members; this implied that the backbench councillor would sit on one, or at the most two committees. Would not the backbench councillor know less of the operations of his authority than at present? Certainly he would be separated from financial administration. In this situation could a council be expected to scrutinise effectively the decisions of its management board?

Possibly the gravest criticism is contained in the Report itself in a note of dissent by one of the members of the Maud Committee, Sir Andrew Wheatley. While accepting the concept of the management board, Sir Andrew argued that committees must be given wider scope than that allowed to them in the Committee's plan. He feared that the management board might become too autocratic and remote from other members of a council and that this would damage the essential democratic quality of our local government.

He also argued that if backbench members of a local council were limited to a minor advisory role there would not be a sufficient incentive for able people to come forward and offer themselves as candidates at local elections. To serve on a committee without executive responsibilities is a sure prescription for frustration. As an alternative, therefore, Sir Andrew proposed that committees be given some executive powers; while they should always consult with the management board they should, in case of disagreement, report direct to the council. This view has much to commend it, but such disagreement would be highly unlikely in any authority run on strict party lines: it is relevant also that party influence is increasing steadily and will become more pronounced now that local authorities are fewer and larger.

The Maud Committee gave very full consideration to the impact of party politics in local government. On one matter they wished to depart from the national government model because they argued that minority parties should be represented on the management board. The Leader of the Opposition is not a member of the Cabinet! Ideally, members on a local council from all parties should be able to contribute to the good management of public affairs. Much of local administration is, or ought to be, essentially non-political in character. And unless minority supporters could have an opportunity to serve on the management board, there would be a break in continuity and a lack of experience whenever the party majority on a council changed. Even so, it is difficult to see how a local political 'cabinet' can effectively discuss controversial matters if their leading opponents are always present. There was no suggestion that the management board should be a 'coalition government'. Minority representation also implies that the management board as a whole would not be responsible for the conduct of affairs but solely those members who belong to the local majority party.

Not one local authority accepted the Maud scheme *in toto*. Yet many were stimulated to streamline their committee structures and to nominate one or more major co-ordinating committees. If the idea of the management board went beyond what was currently acceptable in local government circles, it also had an important educational effect and helped to pave the way for the rather less radical Bains Report of 1972. Largely because of Maud, the Bains Committee worked within a situation where the need for reform in administrative methods was already widely accepted.

The Bains Report was more flexible in its approach to management structures: it agreed that there was no ideal model on which a local authority should operate. It argued that the functions of councillors and officials were not separable into watertight compartments and that the nature of a councillor's interest in administration also varied between individuals. Some were mainly attracted to welfare work; others to restricting expenditure; others to management, often on commercial lines; others in general service to the community. The Report added 'Other categories can no doubt be identified', but was too tactful to proceed further. It follows from this analysis that councillors will want to fill different roles in their public duties. Some are keen to be involved in major questions of policy, resource allocation and management. Others are content to be occupied with more detailed committee work.

The Report followed what has become normal doctrine in urging that a local authority should have a senior or central committee, advised by a Chief Executive, to formulate policy on major issues and generally oversee all the authority's activities. Unlike the Maud management board, the Bains central policy committee was not to have a monopoly of policy-making because some decisions were to be left with functional committees. A central policy committee should frame a comprehensive plan to govern priorities in expenditure which should be revised regularly. It was important that previous decisions should not be regarded as immutable. The Report stressed that more attention should be paid to the effectiveness of local government services: in the past tools of measurement had concentrated on expenditure, on input into a service, rather than its output. This prescription is splendid in theory. Yet how can it be applied in practice? Education is the most expensive local function: here is the greatest opportunity to check efficiency by improving output. But how do you measure output of a school or college—by examination results? Any attempt to proceed on these lines would be reminiscent of the eighteen-sixties: it would invoke overwhelming opposition from educationalists. Output of clerical and manual employees engaged on mainly routine tasks can be subjected to some form of measurement, but to apply similar checks to professional and managerial staffs cannot adequately assess, and would probably damage, the *quality* of their work. The Bains Committee did not really face up to these problems. Its keenness to promote efficiency at the very highest levels of administration is still praiseworthy. There was to be no soft or quiet life for those in top jobs. It doubted whether every chief officer needed a deputy. And it produced the radical notion that chief officials should be subject to an annual appraisal of their performance by a sub-committee of the policy committee advised by the Chief Executive; the latter should be similarly appraised by the policy committee itself.

A central Policy and Resources Committee was the main feature of the Bains model for local authority management. Four sub-committees were also recommended to deal with finance, staff, land and a general review of performance in relation to objectives. It was emphasised that these sub-committees should not concern themselves with trivial questions of expenditure but should think in broad terms about major issues. The Policy Committee should not consist solely of chairmen of other committees; it should include 'backbench' councillors and some drawn from political minorities. So it would not be so much of a Cabinet as the Maud-style management board. There would be a less sharp distinction between inner-group councillors who serve on the Policy Committee and those who do not. The pattern of other committees should be related to the objectives of a council rather than to the organisation of particular services: thus committee structure need not follow departmental structure. When major decisions have to be made, committees should consider alternative means of reaching their objectives. Not surprisingly the Bains Report saw no virtue in area sub-committees operating within a scheme of delegated authority, for such bodies do not assist managerial efficiency. However, where an authority covers a wide area of countryside, there is likely to be pressure, not merely for decentralised access to services, but also for decentralised decisions so that county administration can become more sensitive to local needs and opinion. The Report did accept that, in some cases, services would have to operate through local offices and it recommended that such offices should cover areas which corresponded with district council boundaries.

The Bains Committee saw no need to insist that the Chief Executive should have any specific qualification: this recommendation leaves the field for recruitment wide open. Nor, the Bains Report argued, should he have an official deputy—a proposal that invites an awkward hiatus if the Chief Executive should become ill, die, resign or otherwise disappear. The intention was that the Chief Executive should have no specific departmental responsibilities so that his desk and his mind should be left clear to deal with major items of policy. The Bains proposal was that the traditional legal and administrative duties of the Clerk be transferred to a new type of chief officer—the Secretary of a local authority. Not all councils have adopted the view that their Chief Executive should be spared departmental cares. It can be argued that if the top administrator sits apart in semi-isolation he will find it more difficult to keep in touch with contemporary problems; that without a department to support him he lacks eyes and ears to tell him what is taking place throughout the whole organisation. A remedy for the threatened isolation is to give the Chief Executive a small personal staff and research staff. Of course, such appointments involve added expense and there is still a

tendency in local government to think of research as an unnecessary luxury. The real danger of a central research unit is that it
may be given work better undertaken within the specialised departments.

The Bains theory was that the Chief Executive would promote
co-ordinated decision-making through the assistance of a management team, a kind of Cabinet of officials, formed from the more
important chief officers. The existence of the management team
should be formally recognised by the council. Inter-disciplinary
teams of officials should be formed to advise the various committees.
This suggestion and the parallel recommendation that committee
responsibilities should not be allocated on a simple functional basis
were both designed to check the tendency for local administration to
develop separate departmental empires and loyalties based on the
provision of particular services. To put the matter in the more
formal language used in the Report—there should be a corporate
approach to management rather than a departmental approach.

It may be useful to bring these ideas together, as far as possible,
in diagrammatic form. Below is illustrated the Bains model for the
committee structure of a non-metropolitan county. The crucial issue
is the relationship between the Policy Committee and the other
main committees. It appears that the task of the Policy Committee
was to be less than control. It was to advise the council on the merits
of programmes submitted by other committees: the Bains scheme
mentions concurrent reports to the full council. The idea was that
the Policy Committee should co-ordinate rather than command.
The practice, no doubt, will vary from place to place. Where political
organisation is strong a Policy Committee must reflect the views of
(the leaders of) the majority group, and it can be assumed that other
committees and sub-committees will adjust themselves to carry out
the political programme of the majority party.

Alternative patterns for departmental structure were suggested by
the Bains Report. The simpler arrangement was that each chief
officer would organise his own department and be independent,
subject to co-ordination by the management team—of which he
might not be a member—and by the Chief Executive and, of course,
the ultimate control of the local council. The other pattern grouped
certain departments together under a Director. One such grouping
could be education, libraries and amenities and recreation. Another
could be planning, transport, engineering, architecture, valuation
and estates all placed under a Director of Technical Services. Multi-
departmental directors would belong to the management team but
would be subject to co-ordination in the same way as other chief
officers.

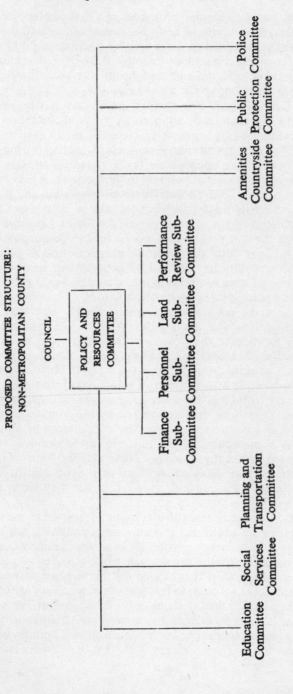

PROPOSED COMMITTEE STRUCTURE:
NON-METROPOLITAN COUNTY

COUNCIL

POLICY AND RESOURCES COMMITTEE

Education Committee

Social Services Committee

Planning and Transportation Committee

Finance Sub-Committee

Personnel Sub-Committee

Land Sub-Committee

Performance Review Sub-Committee

Amenities Countryside Committee

Public Protection Committee

Police Committee

Models based on similar principles can easily be constructed for non-metropolitan districts and the metropolitan authorities. The Bains Report suggested that the smaller districts might have as few as three functional committees dealing with housing, development and leisure services, and environment health. In such places all chief officers would belong to the management team.

The Bains Report was highly influential partly because it reflected concepts already adopted by many of the more vigorous and forward looking authorities. A criticism is that the Report ignored the element of party politics in local government. But would it have been appropriate for a group of officials to make recommendations about political organisation? Again, the style of local political conventions is so diverse that an attempt to prescribe a single mould for them would be both unrealistic and undesirable. A great advantage of the Bains proposals is that they were not too precise and could readily be adapted to meet local situations. But the idea of corporate management may work less smoothly in a period of contraction. In an optimistic atmosphere of expanding horizons, separate departments may be happy to come together to plan the future. If the dominant issue is how to make economy cuts, then officials may look to their own committees for protection. As for the councillors, the question is whether they can see their own role in sufficiently broad terms. Can they get accustomed to thinking in terms of objectives, priorities and programme review? How easy will it be for them to work with the sort of information that is an essential preliminary to taking decisions of this type? Councillors, especially new councillors, feel frustrated by the long-term nature of major local government programmes; they feel hemmed in by what has been decided in the past and often decided by central government rather than the local council. The Maud Committee demonstrated that many councillors were more comfortable with the relatively trivial agenda items because they were easier to comprehend.

Some councillors resent the concept of corporate management because it causes additional and unnecessary expense. Also they feel it increases the influence of officials to an undesirable extent. There can be no doubt that if senior staff work together to produce co-ordinated advice, then that advice will be very persuasive. The less able councillors may come to feel that the bureaucracy are controlling policy. In practice, the influence of the Management Team will vary in its extent. Where a council has a party political majority, and the majority group has effective leaders, then council opinion will remain powerful. Some chief officers feel that corporate management undermines their personal responsibility for their own department. Management teams work differently; many aspects of their activities are unclear. What is the relationship between the Chief Executive and the other members of a Management Team? Is the Chief Executive the equivalent of a President of the United States in that he can overrule all the advisers in his Cabinet? Or is the Chief Executive to act more in the mould of a British Prime Minister who, while having great influence, can ultimately be overborne by his Cabinet colleagues? What is the strength of a decision by a Management Team? Is it collectively binding on the members or can they go away and give confidential advice, say, to their committee chairman, in opposition to the corporate decision? Can the interests of a department not directly or permanently represented on the Management Team be fully safeguarded? If a chief officer presents proposals or information to the Management Team will his committee chairman know what he is doing? All these items are potentially delicate issues. There is no uniformity in the manner in which they are resolved. In many councils a lot of the questions are never asked, at least in public.

MODERN TECHNIQUES OF MANAGEMENT

There is a third broad aspect of the quest for efficiency in local government which covers the various techniques that have been developed to improve and monitor the output of office and outdoor staff. They involve investigation combined with an element of numerical analysis. Processes of this type can also be used to organise information to aid decision making of the kind discussed above. The following paragraphs give an outline of these methods, their uses and their limitations.

The concept of work-study originated in industry. It is concerned with the examination of productive processes to improve efficiency, and developed a number of aspects including the design of machines and equipment, the lay-outs of working areas, and the pattern of labour organisation. The introduction of any bonus incentive payment usually involves some element of work measurement in order to define a norm that must be exceeded if additional payment is to be made; such measurement is another function of the work-study expert. Organisation and methods work is rather more recent in origin and developed in the Civil Service during the last war in response to the need to save manpower and limit administrative expenditure. It concentrated on the use of office machines, the design and simplification of forms and, in general, re-examined the need for traditional administrative practices. It also looked into the distribution of functions between government departments. O and M work, as it is popularly called, has thus a similar purpose to work-study, and the distinction between the two is increasingly blurred.

In local government interest in O and M activity developed in the nineteen-fifties. Elected members of local authorities welcomed it as a possible means of cutting expenditure fairly painlessly and so reducing the demand on the ratepayer. Some of the younger and more ambitious local government officers saw O and M as providing a new and stimulating career opportunity. Many of the larger local authorities have appointed their own O and M officers and the second-tier London Boroughs combined to establish a joint O and M unit. Elsewhere local authorities called in the services of business efficiency consultants, who normally are engaged by private firms to advise how their organisation and profitability could be improved. The use of consultants in local government did not always have happy results. Since their fees were high it was apparent that money would be wasted, not saved, unless their reports showed the way to significant economies. Other difficulties were caused because sometimes they were unfamiliar with local government law, traditions and practice. And whether or not business consultants are used for this work, it is generally true that there has been more resistance in local government to O and M activity than in the Civil Service. This is not surprising. The Civil Service is such a vast organisation that it is unlikely that any single O and M report will significantly affect career prospects of established staff and any redundancies can be smoothed over by moving people on to other duties or by dismissing temporary staff. Local authorities, being much smaller administrative units, do not provide such good opportunities for redeployment of staff. But resistance to O and M activity arises for other reasons. A crucial issue is how far-reaching should an O and M investigation be? Should it be limited to the pattern of office processes—or should it extend to the committee structure of an authority, to the division of responsibility between departments of a local authority, to the relations between committees and officers and, in particular, to how far decisions should be delegated by elected representatives to paid officials? These are fundamental questions which some councillors and some officials would prefer to avoid. Yet any management survey is emasculated if a local authority regards its *modus operandi* as being beyond reproach. Just occasionally friction has also arisen over the question of how much publicity should be given to O and M reports. Some councillors put the argument like this: if public money is spent to enquire into the efficiency of our authority, then the public are entitled to know the full results of the enquiry. But it is generally accepted that establishment matters, as they affect individuals, should remain confidential. Of course, should an O and

M report suggest a basic reorganisation of departments or a reshaping of committees, then some public discussion must take place.

Operational research involves the study of routine tasks by specialists skilled in scientific observation who are usually expert statisticians. The idea is that an essentially mathematical investigation can provide valuable information that will act as a guide towards making the best possible decisions. A few examples will help to demonstrate the kind of problems that can be submitted to this type of examination. Invoices are normally checked to ensure that they are correct both in terms of arithmetic and as a record of goods received. But checking invoices costs money. How far would it be economical in any office to save the cost of checking and bear the risk of loss through inaccuracies going undetected? In any store, whether of materials needed in construction or in a store of office materials, the problem arises of how large an order to place for any item in regular demand. Infrequent ordering of large quantities saves time and trouble and may offer discounts for purchase in bulk, but large stocks demand larger storage space and involve spending money before it is absolutely necessary. What point on the scale between infrequent big orders and many small orders will give the best results? A proportion of outside staff employed on refuse collection is always absent from work for sickness or other reasons; if a refuse collection service is to be constantly regular some surplus labour will have to be employed to make up for the absentees. How much surplus labour is necessary to give a guarantee of regular collection? These are the type of questions to which operational research is applied. It is not possible, of course, within the confines of a short book on local government to explain the mathematical techniques which are used in the solution of such problems.

This sort of research is not an infallible magic that can always lead the way to the best possible decision. Major decisions usually involve judgements which may be of a political nature or simply raise the issue of how much people are prepared to pay to achieve a certain quality of service. Let us revert to the example of refuse collection. A piece of operational research might show that if 20 per cent more dustmen are employed above the number required if all men were always on duty, then the chances of maintaining regular collection are about 99 per cent. But a council might well take the view that they were prepared to face a higher risk of irregular collection rather than bear the cost of the additional labour involved. Or to revert to the case of invoice checking, a council might not be willing to reduce standards of internal auditing because of the visitations of the District Auditor. But operational research can provide a firm basis of information on which decisions can be made. Without such impersonal investigation decisions on administrative methods will be made on the basis of hopes, hunches or traditions, i.e. a problem is dealt with in a particular way simply because it was handled like that in the past when, quite possibly, conditions of scale or cost were quite different.

Cost-benefit analysis is another technique that has been developed to aid decision-making. This is more usually applied to projected future capital developments. If there are alternative schemes for highway development, the more expensive providing for freer, faster and perhaps safer traffic flow, which should be chosen? The idea of cost-benefit analysis, put simply, is to estimate the costs and benefits of alternative plans and to demonstrate their relative advantages. Here again there are substantial difficulties. Any estimate of future benefit must be hypothetical to some degree. Some benefits cannot be quantified or translated into monetary terms, e.g. a design for a road or a building may be aesthetically more pleasing than a cheaper design, but one cannot make a scientific estimate of the benefit to be derived from beauty. And when an analysis is completed there remains the basic value judgement of how much we are prepared to contribute now to benefit the next generation. This can be illustrated again in terms of highway development. Given certain expectations of the growth of motor traffic, a relatively modest scheme of highway improvement may be thought adequate to meet the needs of the next decade while a more elaborate scheme would be adequate for a much longer period. Which scheme should be adopted? Cost-benefit analysis cannot answer this problem. It can provide material upon which a more informed judgement can be made in that people can be made aware of the probable consequences of any decision.

This new emphasis on research and quantification as a preliminary to the taking of decisions has increased the need to carry out complex calculations with speed and accuracy. The growth of local authority administration also demands that routine office work be mechanised as far as possible. Together these requirements have produced a rapid increase in the use of computers in local government; many large councils have installed their own machine and often arrange to share their use with neighbouring authorities. A computer is a highly sophisticated piece of electronic technology. Only a limited number of specialists understand fully how they work. But it will be necessary for an increasing number of administrators to know what computers can do to help their work and, indeed, to know how to give instructions to the machines. Hence the very great interest in systems analysis and computer programming. Applications of the new technology are developing steadily: some of their most common uses are for regular payments of all kinds, e.g. wages and interest charges, the preparation of election registers, data storage and the analysis of expenditure and income, of costing, and of statistics relating to planning applications, traffic flows, housing lists and education.

The growth of interest among local authorities in management techniques has led them to appoint specialised staff to develop their applications. In addition, with the encouragement of financial help from the central government, a national agency has been formed to give assistance to local councils. This body is LAMSAC, Local Authorities Management Services Advisory Committee; it issues advice to authorities based on detailed research and also provides a confidential consultancy service for individual authorities. Problems dealt with include the desirability of installing a computer, changing an existing computer, or how to introduce job evaluation on incentive bonus schemes. LAMSAC has established groups to investigate some management aspect of every major local function. All this work obtains little publicity. It also faces the obstacle that if improved administrative methods reduce workload then the contentious issue of redundancy emerges. Economies may be achieved by not filling vacancies and by redeployment. But, in a period of high unemployment, there is less labour mobility so there is less possibility of cutting staffing costs painlessly. A major attraction of management studies has been that they promised to reduce expenditure. However, because of understandable trade union pressure, this promise may not be fulfilled.

Meanwhile, there is a widespread public belief that local authorities are not as efficient as they could or should be. A management expert based within an organisation may well hesitate to bring forward suggestions that are unpalatable to his colleagues. To have bite, a management review must come from outside. For this reason, as noted in the following chapter, the Layfield Report urged that local audit be reorganised.

Chapter VIII

LOCAL GOVERNMENT AND SOCIETY

THE PATTERN OF PRESSURES

It is important to visualise local government in the context of the sum total of its social relationships. This can be assisted by means of a diagram. The chart on the next page is a sort of map which shows how a local authority fits in with the public, with central government, with political parties and other voluntary organisations. It shows the flow of pressure and experience between these parts of the social system—the channels through which demands are made upon a local council, how the council itself may try to exert influence, how the council's services may arouse public reaction and how central government agencies help to supervise local services. Inevitably the diagram involves much simplification. It omits some links which are not immediately significant for the individual local authority. A chart cannot demonstrate the complex relationship within the council organisation between elected members and officers. But it does show the essential circularity of local administration—how people make demands on local authorities and subsequently react to how their demands are met. The chart is also able to distinguish those formal relationships which are enshrined in law. Statutory relationships are indicated by a continuous line and informal ones by a broken line. Most of these links operate on a two way basis, e.g. the local authority associations have an effect on Government policy but the Government also has an impact on the attitudes of the associations. It may sometimes be a matter of doubt which is having the greater influence on the other. Thus while local opinion may conceivably take note of the speeches of councillors acting as local opinion leaders, the constitutional position is that the voters choose councillors to represent local opinion.

It should be remembered that the diagram is purely *descriptive*. It does nothing to explain what sort of decision a council will make in any given set of circumstances. This is because it is not possible to quantify pressures or to assess precisely the effect of influences pulling in opposite directions. The diagram is merely an aid to understanding the social situation within which local government must work. In particular it illustrates how various voluntary organisations can have an impact on local administration. The churches are

among the most important of these bodies; in the past they had a dominating position in relation to education. The Lord's Day Observance Society may be stung into action if a local authority arranges or permits some activity on a Sunday. Tenants associations are today among the most vigorous local groups and may organise protests if council house rents are increased. And there are a mass of other bodies urging a wide variety of policies on local authorities: progress in education, anti-fluoridation, rural preservation and so on. The interest of voluntary organisations in local government appears to be growing. They are a peculiarly valuable element in maintaining a spirit of local democracy as they frequently promote causes that cut across the lines of political party policies.

At least two other aspects of the chart demand comment. It shows that the local council decides policy in relation to local services, but it must not be forgotten that the experience of being a member of a local authority and gaining knowledge about local government functions may itself influence members of local councils. A new councillor may think that better standards of service should be provided; after some months on the council he may change his view as he comes to appreciate the financial and other difficulties. Alternatively, a new councillor may be critical of policies he feels to be extravagant; on a fuller acquaintance with the benefits derived from these policies he may come to accept that they are justified. The chart also implies that local experience of local services has an influence on behaviour at elections; if voters are satisfied with the services they will be content to keep the same councillors—otherwise they will seek to make changes. This is the way in which local democracy is supposed to work. In earlier years the theory may have had some connection with practice. Now wherever politics dominates local elections, voters react on party lines according to their views on the performance of the national government. So there may be a big change in the membership and political balance of a local authority, not because of dissatisfaction with the policies or the quality of its administration but because of reactions to Government activity.

VIRES AND DISTRICT AUDIT

The basic legal constraint on local authorities is the doctrine of *ultra vires* which requires them to be able to provide specific legal authorisation for all their actions. The principle was not imposed on local government by a deliberate act of national policy; it evolved from judicial decisions which limited the activities of railway companies to business directly connected with the running of a railway. The argument was that railways were authorised by Acts of Parliament and, as statutory corporations, they must be restricted to the purposes for which they were created. Local authorities were immediately involved because they are all statutory corporations, apart from boroughs outside London. Whether provincial boroughs were also governed by the *ultra vires* rule has become a wholly academic question since, under the 1972 Act, all local authorities are statutory authorities. So local government is fettered by a legal rule that has not received specific authorisation from Parliament: it is, moreover, a rule that the Courts have interpreted very strictly.

There can, of course, be two views on the desirability of the *ultra vires* principle. Certainly, it inhibits enterprise and experiment; it also removes opportunities for extravagance and folly. Were councils freed from this restraint they would still be subject to the ballot-box and if electors were not satisfied by the reasons offered for inflated rate-demands a change of councillors and council policy would become highly likely. A few adventures or misadventures by local authorities could rapidly reduce public apathy about their activities. One has the feeling, however, that the *ultra vires* principle is now widely accepted by Ministers, Parliament, local officials and councillors with a certain sense of relief in that it prevents unorthodoxy and fresh difficulties. Optional activities are normally those which cause the greatest friction, partly because they provide obvious targets in any economy drive and partly because their continuation depends wholly on the will of the local council, and there is no possibility of pushing off responsibility on to the central government. Some local disputes about cultural expenditure have attracted widespread publicity. In the nineteen-twenties Labour Members of Parliament supported a Local Authorities (Enabling) Bill which sought to give larger local authorities discretionary powers to promote trading and cultural activities. Yet subsequent Labour Governments have shown no enthusiasm whatever for this sort of legislation. The issue seemed to be dead. However, the 1972 Act allows a local authority, other than a parish meeting, to incur expenditure up to a rate of two new pence for any purpose which in its opinion would benefit its area, provided that such activity is not subject to other statutory provisions. This element of freedom should be further extended by the 1973 property revaluation and the increase of rateable values. Especially for parish and community councils, now treated for this purpose equally with other authorities, the restraint of *ultra vires* has been greatly weakened.

The Maud Committee suggested that a further relaxation be allowed so that local authorities be given a 'general competence' to do whatever they feel to be in the interests of their areas, subject to not encroaching on the spheres of other public bodies and to 'appropriate safeguards for the protection of public and private interests'. The proposal appeared radical but was also extremely vague. The idea of safeguarding private interests could inhibit any scheme to undertake commercial activities; even cultural and recreational provision could conflict with existing business interests. There would also be wide-spread objection to any right to subsidise local political or religious organisations. However, some foreign countries do have 'general competence' clauses. The idea has obvious attractions and could do much to enliven local government. But there are great difficulties in the way of giving this plan a precise legal form.

Although the 1972 Act did not include a general competence clause, it did limit substantially the scope of district audit. The traditional objection to this system was that it empowered a govern-ment official—albeit one independent of Ministers and exercising a quasi-judicial function—to impose penalties on elected representa-tives for using their judgement on how best to serve the interests of their electors. And surcharges were not merely on illegal expenditure but on expenditure held to be unreasonable. Under the 1972 Act district audit is concerned only with legality, not with reasonableness. Further, it no longer imposes penalties for presumed illegality; it has to ask a court of law to do so. Local authorities outside London can manage to avoid district audit by opting to employ professional audit, subject to the right of the Secretary of State to order district audit to make a special investigation into particular accounts. The objection now to the audit system is not that it is anti-democratic, but that it may involve much delay in settling a local controversy. Thus if a professional auditor issues a critical report on some items of local expenditure and this leads to further investigation by district audit which leads to a legal action, the time taken to dispose of the affair will be very considerable.

Today the district auditor seems much less of an ogre. The hostility from fifty years ago has gone. This is well illustrated by the relatively small number of councils which in 1974 chose to evade his attentions by resort to professional audit. Perhaps the district auditor is less sinister because there is less need for him to be so. Local authorities are now conditioned to accept central directions through a wide range of administrative controls, and so are less likely to engage in unorthodox spending. Political conflicts over local government expenditure are not so acute as in the nineteen-twenties —except perhaps in relation to council house rents. Also, instead of initiating legal action, he may give a private warning that certain expenditure is questionable and should not be repeated. He is required to report to authorities on any discrepancies found in the accounts. He can still criticise publicly the financial policy of a council. Such a report might provoke a ratepayer to initiate legal action against a council on the grounds that certain actions were *ultra vires*. To anyone who complains that the reduced role of district audit removes a potent check on local councils it seems fair to reply that there is more danger of local government being choked by too many controls than there is of it running riot through lack of restraints.

The Layfield Committee sought to strengthen the audit service, not in the context of checking *ultra vires* activities but as an aid to efficiency. At present the auditor is required to look for 'loss arising from waste, extravagance, inefficient financial administration, poor value for money, mistake or other cause'. The Layfield Report felt that this instruction was not fully carried out because the auditors were more concerned with the accounts than the realities, in particular the methods of management, that lay behind the accounts. So the Report proposed that the audit should be reorganised as a service independent of central or local government which would report either to a parliamentary committee or to a body representative of local authorities as a whole. Such a reform could bring a new and more dynamic scrutiny into local administration and implies the elimination of professional audit. It would offer a new form of accountability to the public.

CENTRAL-LOCAL RELATIONS

There is no generally accepted theory of central-local relationships. Two contrasting patterns are regularly promoted. One is a partnership of colleagues in a joint enterprise; the other is a principal/agent arrangement in which local authorities act at the behest of their national masters. Both patterns illustrate an aspect of the truth. Local services are organised by the local councils; without their co-operation the central government could not ensure the smooth running of these services, at least in the short run. Again, Ministers are usually willing to listen to advice from local authorities because of their practical experience and knowledge of local conditions. On the other hand, local councils depend for their powers on national legislation and some local government law is certainly shaped on the principal and agent framework, notably the provisions for education and the social services. Ministers tend to speak in terms of partnership when they want to be tactful and in terms of principal and agent whenever they wish to enforce a particular policy.

The development of political controversy in relation to local affairs has also tended to link central and local government more closely together. This is not simply a matter of national parties contesting local elections or of the control of a council's policy by the 'caucus' of the local majority party. It is also the case that Ministers often claim political credit for the activities of local authorities, especially in connection with building houses and schools, in spite of the fact that a large part of this construction has been carried out by councils dominated by their political opponents. Ministers also press the development of certain policies that affect the way local authorities carry out their responsibilities, e.g. green belt preservation, council house rents, the sale of council houses and, not least, comprehensive secondary education.

It is often argued that such ministerial influence is undemocratic in that the wishes of locally elected representatives can be overridden by the edict of a remote organisation in Whitehall. Yet this argument is not easy to sustain. If democracy is defined as the acceptance of majority opinion, it would seem to be as democratic to follow the will of the Minister who represents the national majority as it is to follow the wishes of those who represent but a local majority. If democracy is defined in terms of paying attention to local opinion, then the smaller the unit of opinion the more attention should be paid to its desires. Should a parish council be allowed to override a county council? Should the representatives of a ward be entitled to insist that a different policy be applied to their ward as opposed to the other wards in the borough? Financial considerations apart, claims of this sort are a prescription for anarchy. Here is a dilemma. A healthy democracy needs strong, vigorous and independent-minded local government genuinely able to exercise initiative and judgement. At the same time local authorities get massive monetary aid from the Treasury and are expected to assist in promoting national social purposes.

The independence of local authorities has been deeply undermined by their reliance on financial help from the central government. The rating system is now under such severe attack that its continued existence is uncertain. There is no doubt that local rates are a most unsatisfactory form of taxation for there is no certain correlation, as there is with income tax, between the amount an individual has to pay and his capacity to pay. Resistance to paying higher rates, aggravated by the unfairness of the system, has effectively reduced the taxing capacity of local councils and has led to incessant demands for more state subsidies. It is widely argued that education —easily the most expensive local government service—is a national service and, as such, should be financed entirely by the national Exchequer. Yet how far would it continue to be a local government service if education authorities had no financial responsibility save to the Secretary of State for Education? Meanwhile, local control of administration and expenditure, albeit constrained by Whitehall, does preserve an element of community responsibility, pride and satisfaction. Services provided by the central government do not inspire similar attitudes. Compare the health service to local welfare services. There is general dissatisfaction with the hospital service—not necessarily with the individual contributions of doctors, nurses and hospital administrators—but with the scale of provision as a whole. There is a feeling that 'they', the anonymous, abstract and unknown controllers of the system, ought to effect various improvements. Controllers of the local welfare services are not unknown; if there are serious complaints, they will soon hear of them. Where cost is the obstacle to meeting the complaint, the difficulty is more readily appreciated. 'To improve the welfare services means putting the rate up' is a statement which carries a more meaningful choice than 'To improve hospitals means an increase in taxation.' It is not merely that the national purse may appear bottomless, it is also the case that any successful local claim on national resources has a net benefit to the local community. So long as cost is linked to a local tax, the cost-benefit relationship is realistic. Whenever the Government takes over a local service it puts a premium on grumbling by destroying local financial responsibility. Further, the nineteenth-century desire to achieve minimum standards throughout the country in relation to vital services such as poor relief and education has tended to develop into the imposition of maximum standards and, indeed, to an overall regime of uniformity. As local authorities receive so much financial aid this equality of provision is easily justified on grounds of fair distribution of the national taxpayer's money.

Lack of revenue is not the sole economic cause of greater central supervision. As a major public consumer of labour and capital resources, local government is required to keep in step with the changing face of the Government's economic policy. Wages and salary levels of local authorities will be influenced by any national incomes policy: the nature and extent of capital expenditure on local schools, housing, roads, swimming baths, etc. will have to fit broadly into a national scheme of priorities. All public bodies are expected to co-operate in freezes and squeezes or any other general measures that Ministers feel necessary to promote the national economic interest.

Whenever there is pressure to reduce spending, the tendency is to cut capital projects rather than current expenditure. This is a natural reaction because new construction implies some improvement of service while a cut in current expenditure normally means a lowering of existing standards. If the choice is between fresh ventures and the preservation of what has already been achieved, then the latter may seem the more prudent course of action. Yet the axe falls on capital schemes also because this alternative avoids redundancy for local authority staff and thus avoids trouble with trade unions. The result is some lack of flexibility of local policy which may prevent the optimum use of resources. New needs can be sacrificed for past needs that are no longer as strong as they once were.

Further, the concept that the flow of capital works can be turned off and on like a tap—to suit the contemporary economic climate—suffers from serious limitations. Construction plans take time to prepare—planning enquiries and compulsory purchase orders may be involved. Construction works take time to complete. So it is impossible to commence projects that are not yet ready to start: it is wasteful to slow down or stop projects that are nearing completion. Capital programmes are now worked out two or three years in advance and acquire a momentum of their own. Indeed, a political party that gains a majority at Westminster or in a local council chamber will find that the rigidity imposed by capital schemes, already in hand or about to commence, can be so great as to frustrate the introduction of new policies which involve construction work.

The status of local government has been eroded in this century both by local weakness and by the development of a highly centralised form of public administration. Local weakness is financial and also a matter of organisation and personnel. The traditional committee system was better designed for promoting discussion than for promoting leadership. The reformed structure and streamlined committee organisation will make for improvement but they also impose a heavy burden on many councillors, especially committee chairmen. Some chairmen have the necessary time, ability and vigour to take full command of the business of their committees. Others—probably a majority—lack one or more of these essential qualities. With chief officers increasingly conditioned to think in terms of efficient management rather than adventurous policies, it is almost inevitable that, with exceptions, local councils conform to a national trend and do not take exciting initiatives. Meanwhile the advantage of the central government is the product of powerful interlocking factors: a country that is densely populated but relatively small in area; the cultural, financial and political supremacy of London; the firmly entrenched two-party system that gives the Cabinet a secure parliamentary majority; the acceptance by both parties of welfare policies which they are determined to control nationally.

The Maud Report on *Management of Local Government* accepted this centralised pattern and proposed to strengthen it still further.

The Government was recommended to see if it were possible to nominate a single Minister to be responsible for co-ordinating its policy in relation to local authorities. The establishment of the Department of the Environment in 1970 went a long way towards meeting this request. The Maud Committee also wanted the establishment of a Local Government Central Office to promote research, operate a central staffing organisation and conduct negotiations with the central government. Such an office would take over a large part of the present functions of the local authority associations. These proposals are a logical step ahead in the further unification of public administration. Yet there is a danger to the creation of a main official channel of communication. It may well be more efficient; it may also become rather remote from the individual local authority. And any agreement reached in this central channel would be difficult to overturn in Parliament or anywhere else.

There is a case for urging that these centripetal forces should be resisted. Strong reasons can be advanced against national intervention in local affairs, notably on matters of detail. Every increase in central control requires more staff in national offices to check what local authorities are doing. Not merely does this cost money but it adds to delay. Each new item in the catalogue of supervision means a further loss of local responsibility. Both councillors and local government officers can plead with some justification that it is not their fault if something goes amiss since they are acting under central direction. Distant control must be frustrating. It can develop a feeling among vigorous and able people that service in local government as elected representatives or salaried officers is not worthwhile. The claim for clear—if limited—independence for local government was stated by the Local Government Manpower Committee in 1950, '. . . local authorities are responsible bodies competent to discharge their own functions and though they may be statutory bodies through which Government policy is given effect and operate to a large extent with Government money, they exercise their responsibilities in their own right, not ordinarily as agents for Government Departments. It follows that the object should be to leave as much as possible . . . to the local authority and to concentrate the Department's control at key points where it can most effectively discharge its responsibilities for Government policy and financial administration.' This type of sentiment attracts some support from politicians, especially when in opposition. In terms of law and practice, the recommendation of the Manpower Committee has been ignored. To take just one example: Section 8 of the Public Libraries and Museums Act, 1964, permits the Secretary of State for Education and Science to decide the scale of fines for books overdue from a public library. It is impossible to provide adequate justification for a control of such a petty nature.

The Town and Country Planning Act, 1968, did constitute a distinct check to the centralising tendency. There is now less detailed Ministry supervision over local development plans and the inspectors who hold planning appeals are empowered to take minor decisions themselves instead of merely preparing recommendations for ministerial consideration. At the same time more emphasis is being placed on the need for local planners to consult local opinion. Why were these changes made? Is it that national administration has greater faith in the wisdom of local authorities? The more realistic explanation is that the highly centralised system of approvals and appeal decisions began to break down through the sheer volume of work. Delays in obtaining Ministry decisions lengthened so greatly that some simplification of the system became inevitable.

The Local Government Act, 1972, removed further detailed controls especially in regard to requirements to appoint certain committees and obtain ministerial approval for certain appointments. This is very welcome. Yet it is important not to be misled about the trend of future central-local relationships. Petty, irritating controls can be removed because other more basic legal and financial restraints are ever-present.

Members of the Layfield Committee on Local Government Finance were acutely aware of the effect on central/local relationships caused by the financial weakness of local councils. They were concerned about the confusion caused by a clear lack of accountability for local authority expenditure. Most local spending is directly related to some statutory obligation imposed by central government. The whole Layfield Report is based on the theme of accountability: it argued that those responsible for causing expenditure should accept the onus of finding the money to meet the bills. If present trends continued this would require central government to accept responsibility for the bulk of local expenditure. Ministers would have to determine broadly how much local authorities should spend and for what purpose. Ministers would provide grants and would also indicate the rate poundage necessary to finance appropriate standards of local service. Some local discretion would still remain. Thus local authorities could provide a better standard of service than that required by central government; for this purpose the local rate would be raised above the level required by central government. Councillors would be responsible for the discretionary element in the rate levy to the local electorate; they would be accountable to the Minister for the efficient conduct of the non-discretionary expenditure.

The Layfield Committee were not happy with the prospect of such developments. They preferred an alternative in which local councils would be free to make their own spending and taxing decisions. Even so, it was admitted that central government would need, in the interests of national economic management, to supervise the total of local spending. (Whether this could be done without interference on matters of detail is questionable.) Certainly, local councils could not attain such financial autonomy without fresh taxing powers. To give them such independence, the Layfield Report proposed the introduction of a local income tax.

Contrasting models for the future development of local government are set out in the two preceding paragraphs; these are sometimes described as the 'centralist' or 'localist' alternatives. Without doubt, the pressure of events is tending to push local government towards the former. Professor Day, in a note of reservation to the Layfield Report, proposed a third alternative or a middle way. His suggestion was that national government should define *minimum* standards for local services and pay for the cost of providing them. Local councils would decide how far they wished to go beyond the national minima and should pay, through local taxation, for whatever they decided to spend. However, local freedom would not be absolute: councils would have to restrict spending within a ceiling imposed by central government in the interests of national economic management. This system would differ from the 'centralist' arrangement because that implied Ministers would determine what the nation could afford: under Professor Day's plan, Ministers would decide upon an acceptable minimum. The Layfield Committee rejected this middle way because it felt there would be grave difficulties in fixing minimum standards and costing them.

How did the Callaghan Government respond to the alternatives posed by the Layfield Committee? Tactfully it stood aside from the localism/centralism conflict and commended the middle way. The Green Paper *Local Government Finance* then argued that the 'middle way' suggestions made by Professor Day were impractical. It followed the familiar theme that the relationship between local and central government must be a partnership, the nature of which would develop over time as conditions change. In fact, the whole force of the Green Paper was to press the centralist case. Ministers, it was argued, must exert greater influence over total local expenditure and sometimes would need extra financial weapons to ensure local adoption of particular policies. This philosophy formed the basis of a scheme described above (p. 106) to reshape the Rate Support Grant in a way which would enable Whitehall to put greater pressure on individual councils to adopt spending programmes agreeable to

Ministers. So the Layfield Report is unlikely to lead to a new dawn of local freedom for initiative. Indeed, local independence is likely to be increasingly throttled by the requirements of macro-economic planning.

COMPLAINTS MACHINERY

The growth of public services has provided much wider facilities for everyone. It has also made life more complicated. How are people to know what their rights are? How are they to discover what opportunities are available? How can they feel reasonably certain that their claims and applications have been handled fairly by public officials?

There are two separate problems here. One is an aspect of the general need for wide dissemination of information about local government: this is discussed in the following section. The other problem is to ensure that the administration of public policy is efficient and fair as between individuals. Whether policy itself is fair can be a matter for political judgement and argument, to be decided by public debate and the ballot-box. The task for public administration is to ensure that current policy is effectively and impartially carried out. National government has felt obliged to appoint a Parliamentary Commissioner or Ombudsman to look into complaints. (Strictly speaking, the use of the word Ombudsman is inappropriate. The Scandinavian Ombudsman, on which our system is based, can initiate legal action against defaulting officials; our Parliamentary Commissioner for Administration does not have this power.) The complaints must be about administration—not policy—and must be forwarded to the Commissioner by Members of Parliament. This machinery was an attempt to overcome an evil of mass society, that the shortcomings of bureaucracy may not always be held in check by the traditional means of parliamentary question and debate. But it was also argued that many matters on which the sense of personal grievance may be greatest, concerning planning, housing, education and welfare provisions, come within the ambit of local government rather than national government. If national civil servants are liable to be investigated by an independent official acting in response to a complaint from an aggrieved person, it seems natural that this practice be extended to local authorities.

Local government already suffers so many checks and restraints that it must be asked whether an extra one is needed. The parallel with central government is far from exact. Local authority administration is on a much smaller scale than national administration and the chance that serious mistakes will go uncorrected should be substantially less. At Westminster the Member of Parliament is physically remote from civil servants; he will not know them personally except by rarest chance; he will scarcely if ever meet them. Traditionally, Members have sent in complaints to Ministers who will have a political, if not a personal, motive for asserting that the administrative processes of their departments are tantamount to perfection. Virtually none of this applies to local government. Councillors know their chief officials and take complaints to them direct. They are, indeed, concerned with the details of administration through their committee work. Do local authorities need Ombudsmen since, in a sense, they have plenty already through the presence of elected representatives? But it is not clear that a councillor can always fill the role of an Ombudsman. If a complaint concerns a decision reached in one of his committees he may be asked to investigate one of his own actions or the consequences thereof. If a councillor does not belong to the relevant committee he may know nothing of the basis on which a decision is made and so is not well placed to make critical enquiries. Further, the time councillors can devote to complaints from the public must be limited by their other commitments. The problem of 'constituency' duties is now more fully recognised. The Bains Report proposed that councillors be provided with secretarial services to help them to carry out this function. Certainly, a councillor should be a first link between an aggrieved individual and local administration—but he may not always provide full protection.

It is vital for democracy that the claims and grievances of citizens be dealt with equitably. This cannot mean that all grievances should be satisfied and all claims accepted. It does require that complaints be reviewed impartially and that where one claim is given preference over another real justification can be found for the decision. Thus if a council house is allocated to Brown rather than to Smith, it must be because Brown has greater need of accommodation, because he has been evicted or is living under more crowded conditions or some similar reason—not because Brown has a friend or relative on the council or because he has bribed an official. In Britain these principles are understood and accepted. There is a tendency to feel that administrative abuses are so rare as not to constitute a problem. While corruption and other patent abuse is infrequent, there are still many cases of administrative error, failure of communication and lack of understanding. Local government does show concern and respect for individuals and is well placed to set an example for central government in these matters because of the smaller, more intimate scale of its operations. However, the reform of local government structure has now given us fewer but larger units of local administration and fewer councillors. The councillor, like the MP, is becoming divorced from administration. All these factors greatly strengthen the case for local Ombudsmen. But five years of discussion and negotiation were required before positive action was taken. The arguments over the form of the new organisation raised important issues.

The Prime Minister, Harold Wilson, accepted the need for such complaints machinery in a statement to the Commons in July 1969. But what form should this machinery take? JUSTICE (the organisation which popularised the Ombudsman idea in relation to central government) subsequently issued detailed proposals. It suggested that Commissioners of Local Administration should be appointed by the Lord Chancellor; that their salaries should be charged to the national Exchequer and that they should work through a single centralised office. Complaints of maladministration would be made to the Commissioners directly by members of the public. A report on each investigation would be sent to the person who initiated the complaint and to the local authority concerned: an Annual Report of the work of the Local Administration Commissioners would be presented to Parliament. It would be for the local authority to decide what action, if any, to take upon an adverse report from the Commissioners. The Labour Government's own proposals were somewhat different: the 1970 White Paper *Reform of Local Government in England* (Cmnd 4276) stressed that the function of local Ombudsmen would be to help councillors to ensure high standards of administration. Complaints would be made via councillors and the Commissioners would report to local councils and not to Parliament. The scheme was to be administered through a body representative of local government and costs would be met from local funds. Thus the complaints machinery would be separated from central government and would not be another facet of central control.

The scheme now in operation was introduced by the Conservatives through the Local Government Act, 1974. It follows in broad outline the earlier Labour proposals. A complaint need not necessarily be made through a councillor but it must have been submitted to the responsible authority which must have had a reasonable chance to investigate and reply to the complaint. England is divided up between the Commissioners, each of whom is responsible for complaints from a particular area. Wales has a separate Commission. Matters excluded from their attention embrace the conduct of schools; personnel matters; anything that took place before 1 April 1974; anything that could be the subject of appeal to a minister or an administrative tribunal; anything for which a remedy could be obtained from a court of law; anything connected with the commercial activities of a local authority or with criminal investigations. The Commissions report on the pattern of their work to national bodies representing local authorities. Investigations into complaints are held in private. Reports on each case are to be made to the parties concerned; these reports mention no names of individuals, but must be available for public inspection. Where a grievance is found to be justified it is for the local authority to decide what remedies should be offered. Any remedy should be notified to the Commissioner who, if not satisfied, could issue a further report. Thus the Commission has no power over the local council: the essence of this safeguard is impartial investigation followed by publicity. But a council that does not respond to criticism by a Local Commissioner could expect a considerable public outcry.

This machinery creates fresh problems. What limits should be placed on matters to be investigated? The Local Commissioners are to enquire, not into policy, but into maladministration. But what exactly is maladministration? One answer is the so-called Crossman catalogue produced by Mr Crossman when introducing to the House of Commons the legislation which authorised the establishment of the national Ombudsman. The catalogue is bias, neglect, inattention, delay, incompetence, ineptitude, perversity, turpitude, arbitrariness. Put more simply, maladministration would seem to cover any situation in which a local official's action has been improper or seriously inadequate. But maladministration does not include the exercise of discretion. For example, if a local authority is empowered to give or to withhold some benefit, a disappointed applicant cannot claim maladministration unless he can demonstrate some fault in the way in which the decision was made.

Local government officers may be worried lest unjustified complaints damage the reputation and career prospects of an innocent party. Will allegations be made by cranks or embittered and malicious people? This possibility is more serious in local government than in central government for the Civil Service is remote and anonymous. Anyone who alleges maladministration against the Civil Service will only rarely know which official is responsible. A local complaint is more likely to have a personal element. The first safeguard for the local official is the law of defamation. A councillor who forwards a complaint to a Local Commissioner and any report by the Commissioner are both privileged, i.e. they cannot be the subject of a libel action. But this protection does not extend to whoever makes the initial complaint. Another safeguard is that Local Commissioners will be fully aware that allegations that come to them may be wholly ill-founded and malevolent. Even so the procedure followed by the Commissioners is open to objection. Statements made by a complainant about an official are not subject to cross-examination by that official or his legal representative. Privacy at enquiries is not the best guarantee that truth will emerge. Officials are not named in the reports of Commissioners but, inevitably, when someone is criticised many people within the local authority will know who is involved.

Another difficulty is that to satisfy the findings of the Commissioners may cost money. This is not simply a matter of paying compensation to an individual who has suffered injustice. Reports from the LCA have criticised delay in repairing a council house suffering from damp; failure to publicise planning applications; failure to prevent the obstruction of footpaths; delay in forcing a private landlord to repair his property. Quicker and more efficient exercise of these duties would cost money. Thus pressure from the LCA can conflict with the Government's desire to curb expenditure.

Only a tiny fraction of complaints result in a finding of maladministration. Many grievances are outside the jurisdiction of the LCA as they fall within the excluded categories noted above; in other cases there is no evidence of maladministration; in a few instances the complaint is withdrawn as a result of informal discussions with the local authority. Planning, housing and education are the subjects that stimulate most concern. There were relatively few complaints about social services which may be a reflection of the relative inability of the clients or consumers to formulate their dissatisfaction. To present effectively a case against a public authority requires literary or verbal skills that not everyone possesses. As noted above, the Commissioners cannot force a local council to offer a remedy where a complaint is found to be justified. However, in the great majority of such cases local councils have taken steps to minimise the grievance. Occasionally, to remedy maladministration would be to cause injustice to someone else. Where planning permission has been given after inadequate scrutiny of the consequences of the proposed development, it would be unreasonable to require the demolition of building carried out with the consent of the local authority. A major shortcoming of the local Ombudsman system is that anyone who secures a finding of maladministration cannot, as a result, seek damages through a county court action. It is arguable that this rule should be altered. A council may offer an *ex gratia* payment as a recompense, but that is inadequate protection. Meanwhile, the administrative competence of the Local Commissioners is open to challenge: the average time taken to complete an investigation is eight months. Surely that is excessive.

PEOPLE AND LOCAL GOVERNMENT

It is a commonplace that we live in a mass society. All major units of social organisation, with the family as the main exception, tend to increase in size. Employers are fewer in number and operate on a larger scale; trade unions are fewer and larger; towns, schools, hospitals, even universities, get bigger. Government departments and local authorities also grow larger. Taken together, all this must have a great psychological impact on the individual. There can be a tendency to feel lost in the crowd, to experience a sense of helplessness in face of major social pressures, to lose interest in community problems, indeed, perhaps to lose part of a sense of responsibility for one's own actions. In a word, a dangerous possibility can develop—some would say has developed—for the individual to become alienated from society as a whole. The public support given to youth organisations and other cultural, social and recreational activities is in some measure a recognition of this danger and an attempt to counteract it.

Local government, as the smallest and most approachable unit in our system of public administration, should be able to play a major role in breaking down the invisible barriers between the individual and society. It is easier to make an impact on local decisions than it is to affect national decisions. An essential aspect of the deterrent which is inherent in the Ombudsman concept is the publicity which will accompany the ultimate report on any case. Publicity could have a greater impact in a local context than it has on Civil Service administration. It could help to lessen the widespread indifference to local government. This apathy was fully demonstrated by the research undertaken by the Government Social Survey for the Maud Committee. Over a quarter of those interviewed by the Survey were unable to name *any* service provided by their borough or district council: in county areas, the position was worse as nearly half the interviewees apparently knew nothing of the county's services. People in London Boroughs and rural districts were the worst informed: in the metropolis men and women are lost in the mass society and in the countryside the county council is not so much impersonal as remote. Under one-fifth of those interviewed by the Social Survey remembered having approached a councillor for advice. This picture of indifference is not surprising. Life is short and the potential range of human endeavour and interest is vast. It is not unreasonable to feel that there are other and better things to do than to concern oneself with the problems of local government. Apathy can be a measure of contentment. If people are satisfied with social conditions why should they bother about them?

But apathy may be caused by alienation and ignorance rather than contentment. The nature of possible improvements may be unknown; when produced they may be warmly appreciated although not widely demanded in advance. If local government is to flourish it must take some trouble to educate those of the public willing to listen. Why not circulate to all households after each election the names and addresses of council members, together with a note of their committee assignments? Anyone who calls in at a council office in search of this information will not always find it is easy to obtain. Under the 1972 Act press and public have a right to attend council and committee meetings unless excluded on a specific occasion. There are personal matters relating to staff and financial details of land and property transactions which should be kept confidential. Access to meetings, however, is not enough. Attempts should be made to explain the major decisions facing a council to the public at large, possibly by issuing local White Papers on the analogy of Government White Papers. Of course, where an issue becomes political it is often better tactics to reach a decision quickly rather than stimulate public argument. Local and regional radio and television stations could do more to provoke interest in council activities. Yet councillors and local government officers often treat the mass communications media with reserve. The press, in particular, are sometimes accused of inadequate and inaccurate reporting or of seeking out trivial but apparently sensational news items. Councillors are sensitive about publicity. Perhaps this is due to a desire to avoid controversy; perhaps it is because misleading information can easily create embarrassment for them and may cause needless anxiety for some members of the public.

Some local authorities have appointed public relations officers. The Bains Report urged that the larger authorities should establish a public relations and information unit; it also recommended that authorities should consider producing an annual report containing not merely a factual record of the authority's services and use of resources but also a statement of plans to cope with present problems. All this should promote public understanding of local government and is to be welcomed. But public relations work can raise delicate issues. If a council is divided on party lines, a public relations officer who secures publicity for council policy can be accused of implicitly supporting the policy of the majority group. This challenge may be most difficult to avoid in relation to the exposition of plans for the future. Should public funds be spent on the dissemination of controversial matter? Some such spending is justified otherwise the public cannot know the details of the controversy—and many burning local issues depend not on general principles but their detailed application.

Zealous public relations work has its dangers. The alternative danger, apathy, is at least equally serious. If unchecked it may lead to deterioration of standards of services and permit the erosion of democratic safeguards. One old saying is worth requoting: the secret of liberty is eternal vigilance. A test that should always be applied to any scheme to improve local services is whether it will increase or reduce links with the public. To give local authorities greater freedom of action in the form of general competence powers or to allow them wider discretion in other ways is to increase their impact on society and should arouse more interest. This is not to argue that the 'democracy' test can be the sole or dominant criterion of policy, but it is an aspect of decision-making that may be given too little weight in face of considerations of administrative convenience.

The Skeffington Report, *People and Planning*, issued in 1969 urged that local planners should do more to take the public into their confidence. Meetings and exhibitions should be held at an early stage of any major planning exercise at which comments and suggestions would be invited from organised groups and individual members of the public. Subsequent meetings should explain the final form of the planning proposals. There is no doubt that local bodies such as Chambers of Trade, residents' associations and amenity associations can play a useful role in this kind of process. Whether the average man in the street can make an impact on the complex and professionalised task of planning is dubious. How far is it meaningful to think of individual participation in local government? A parent can play a useful and vigorous part in a parent-teacher association that is raising money to build a swimming-pool. But this is merely to assist with others in the implementation of accepted policy. To 'participate' alone to try and influence policy is likely to be unsuccessful and frustrating. It is inevitable that participation arrangements always have something of a public relations flavour: if the planners encourage participation then people may be less unwilling to accept the consequences of planning.

More recently there has been doubt about the value of participation schemes. They are expensive and provide an easy target for economy cuts. Their public relations effect is open to challenge; the consequence may be to stir hostility rather than to secure acceptance. In terms of numbers the response is often poor. Those who do express a view tend to be the more articulate members of the middle class whose opinions may not be representative. A councillor or an official who dislikes the outcome of a participation exercise can claim it ignores 'the silent majority'.

The contemporary mood also reduces the chance of any major reform of local government in the 1980s. Disenchantment with the results of the 1974 reorganisation has left a weary sense that change is expensive and that its benefits are often over-estimated. Greater devolution of powers to Scotland and Wales might have had some repercussions in England but, for the present, the likelihood of devolution has faded. In particular, the crushing defeat in the 1979 referendum of the scheme for a Welsh Assembly, with powers to influence Welsh local administration, must mean that this idea is dead for years to come. In 1978 the Labour Government produced plans for Organic Change in local government which were largely concerned with increasing the powers of non-metropolitan districts, especially the nine districts above 200,000 population. They would have the chance to regain responsibility for education and social services. In effect, the largest of the former county boroughs outside the main conurbations were to retrieve much of what they had lost in 1974. As most of them are often controlled by the Labour Party there was a clear political motive behind the suggestion. If implemented the plan would have introduced new complexity into county administration and policy formation. Naturally the Association of County Councils objected strongly. And the return of a Conservative Government meant that the Organic Change theme was buried. However, one aspect of the plan survived. The Conservatives favoured the idea that the planning responsibilities of counties and districts should be clarified to prevent delay and expense caused by overlapping: the general effect was to make districts more independent of county influence over development control.

So there is no great excitement or stimulus to be gained from major changes in structure. The economic situation combined with Government policy implies cuts in services rather than development. At least for a short time the restrictive policies may increase general concern over local issues. People may well be agitated over losing services they have come to take for granted. Does public opinion favour better services and higher rates, or poorer services and lower rates? No doubt, the pattern of attitudes varies from one area to another. Local debate on this issue has been largely stifled by the tendency for central government to bear a high proportion of the cost of local government and by pressure from Ministers to achieve a higher degree of uniformity of local provision.

Whenever there is public agitation about a local issue, the voice of protest often comes either from an *ad hoc* action group or from a Ratepayers' Association or Residents' Association, possibly newly created as a result of the irritation. Political parties seem to be left out. Perhaps the parties are not very sensitive to local feeling. Alternatively, the people who are keen to organise protest may prefer to avoid political organisations in order to try and secure wide, all party support for their cause. Local agitation falls broadly into two categories—complaints about the level of the rates and concern about environmental issues. Large rate increases in 1974 created a flurry of new Ratepayers' Associations but after a while this particular tide of protest began to ebb. Those who are roused to action by their rate demand are not genuinely concerned with local government; when the inevitability of paying is accepted, the fury of the ratepayer dies away. Environmental questions have a longer impact. People interested in preserving the quality of their surroundings will know that this is not a matter for short-term campaigns. Threats of development felt to be unsuitable can arise regularly and provide a series of stimuli that help to sustain interest in an environmental pressure group.

A resurgence of public concern should be welcomed. The educational role of local government is a major support for our whole democratic system. As people come to understand the intricacies of local problems they are better equipped to understand the tasks of national government. The limited but still substantial number of men and women elected to take local government decisions have a fuller appreciation of the responsibilities of Ministers, MPs, judges and senior Civil Servants. Ability to join in the process of government at local level may stir unfortunate feelings of pride and prestige, but it also enhances knowledge and judgement and provides a channel of communication between government and governed without which no democracy can flourish.

Appendix A

SIZE OF LOCAL AUTHORITIES: ENGLAND

(i) London

The Greater London Council serves a population of 7,167,000 a figure which is steadily declining. Its rateable value is approximately £1,900 million. The 32 London Boroughs vary in size from Croydon with a population of 329,000 down to Kingston-on-Thames with 136,000 people. Rateable values in London Boroughs range from £311 million in the City of Westminster to £26 million at Sutton. The City of London remains a unique authority in terms of its constitution and powers but it has only 5,300 residents.

(ii) Metropolitan Counties

Name of County	Population (000s)	Rateable Value £MN
Greater Manchester	2,709	300
Merseyside	1,588	188
South Yorkshire	1,317	124
Tyne and Wear	1,193	116
West Midlands	2,777	386
West Yorkshire	2,083	189

(iii) Metropolitan Districts

Metropolitan County	Number of districts	Population range (000s)	Rateable Value range (£MN)	Largest district
Greater Manchester	10	180–656	18–70	Manchester
Merseyside	5	193–561	20–71	Liverpool
South Yorkshire	4	224–561	16–61	Sheffield
Tyne and Wear	5	171–297	15–37	Newcastle
West Midlands	7	199–1,086	25–155	Birmingham
West Yorkshire	5	194–738	15–78	Leeds

(iv) Non-Metropolitan Counties

English County	Population (000s)	Rateable Value (£MN)	Number of districts
Avon	920	109	6
Bedfordshire	489	71	4
Berkshire	658	106	6
Buckinghamshire	502	81	5

English County	Population (000s)	Rateable Value (£MN)	Number of districts
Cambridgeshire	551	63	6
Cheshire	911	116	8
Cleveland	565	69	4
Cornwall	401	39	6
Cumbria	474	42	6
Derbyshire	887	91	9
Devon	937	100	10
Dorset	573	74	8
Durham	608	51	8
East Sussex	657	89	7
Essex	1,411	205	14
Gloucestershire	488	56	6
Hampshire	1,450	177	13
Hereford and Worcester	586	71	9
Hertfordshire	938	152	10
Humberside	848	88	9
Isle of Wight	111	12	2
Kent	1,445	160	14
Lancashire	1,369	130	14
Leicestershire	836	96	9
Lincolnshire	521	51	7
Norfolk	659	74	7
North Yorkshire	636	60	8
Northamptonshire	505	87	7
Northumberland	287	26	6
Nottingham	983	107	8
Oxfordshire	535	70	5
Salop	355	37	6
Somerset	402	43	5
Staffordshire	995	110	9
Suffolk	570	66	7
Surrey	998	158	11
Warwickshire	472	59	5
West Sussex	623	83	7
Wiltshire	512	52	5

Welsh County	Population (000s)	Rateable Value (£MN)	Number of districts
Clwyd	373	36	6
Dyfed	320	27	6
Gwent	440	41	5
Gwynedd	224	20	5
Mid Glamorgan	540	34	6
Powys	101	8	3
South Glamorgan	392	45	2
West Glamorgan	372	36	4

(v) Non-Metropolitan Districts

The English non-metropolitan districts differ from the other new county and district authorities in that their boundaries were not defined by the Local Government Act, 1972. Instead their boundaries were proposed by the Local Government Boundary Commission for England in their First Report (Cmnd 5148). These proposals were accepted by the Secretary of State and incorporated in Orders submitted for parliamentary approval.

In carrying out its task the Commission had extensive consultations with existing local authorities in order to try and find local solutions that were generally acceptable. It also had to work within the framework of a set of guidelines from the Secretary of State. The guidelines were as follows:

POPULATION, THE COUNTY PATTERNS OF DISTRICTS AND THE IDENTITY OF TOWNS

1. The Boundary Commission should recommend a pattern of districts for the non-metropolitan counties ranging upwards in population from 40,000. Only very exceptionally should a district be proposed with a population under 40,000.
2. Except in sparsely populated areas the aim should be to define districts with current populations generally within the range of about 75,000–100,000. These figures are in no sense absolute limits; some districts will be larger or smaller, according to local circumstances; but regard should be had to the desirability of producing in each county a pattern of districts which are broadly comparable in population and conducive to effective and convenient local government throughout the county as a whole.
3. The identity of large towns should be maintained. The whole designated area of a new town, or the whole of an area defined for town development, should ordinarily fall within one new district.
4. Normally it will be necessary to take only current population levels into account in considering the size of district to be proposed. Account should be taken of a town's engagement in an approved programme of rapid expansion, e.g. under the New Towns Act or Town Development Act, but even in these cases regard must also be had to the population level needed to sustain efficient services in the meantime.

Definition of new districts

5. Wherever reasonably practicable a new district should comprise the whole of one or more existing county boroughs or county districts. Where this is not practicable, the new district should

comprise whole parishes or wards. Because of the need to concentrate on the main pattern of the new districts, new boundaries which do not follow the boundary of an existing local government unit or electoral area should be proposed only in special circumstances. Once the new authorities have taken over, the Commission will be invited to carry out a thorough review of proposals for detailed adjustment of boundaries, including those of the counties and metropolitan districts.

General considerations

6. In formulating their recommendations the Commission should weigh all relevant considerations in the light of the general objectives of local government reorganisation as set out in the Government's White Paper, Cmnd 4584. Among other things they should have particular regard to the wishes of the local inhabitants, the pattern of community life, and the effective operation of local government services.

7. The Commission will also wish to take note of the pattern of Parliamentary constituencies in each county.

Population criteria provided the more important guidelines. However, the Commission ultimately proposed the establishment of 14 districts below the projected minimum of 40,000. Most of these authorities are in sparsely populated areas where the creation of larger authorities would have meant that the district councils were unduly remote. One exception to this rule is Christchurch in Dorset. The original intention here was that Christchurch should be combined with Lymington to form a district council of average size. However, at a very late stage in the parliamentary discussion of the Bill, the House of Lords successfully insisted that Lymington remain in Hampshire, so Christchurch was left to form a district on its own with a population of 33,000. A quite different type of special case is provided by the county of Cleveland where the Government issued a special instruction to the Commission requiring it to divide up the existing county borough of Teesside. This was felt to be essential as otherwise Teesside would have provided two-thirds of the population of the county.

ALLOCATION OF MAIN FUNCTIONS

Non-Metropolitan Counties
Social Services

Education and Related Services
  Education
  Libraries
  Museums and Art Galleries (c)

Housing and Town Development
  Certain reserve powers, e.g. over-
    spill
  Town Development

Town and Country Planning and
    Related Matters
  Structure Plans
  Local Plans (in special cases)
  Development Control (strategic
    and reserved decisions)
  Acquisition and Disposal of Land
  Clearance of Derelict Land (c)
  National Parks (subject to exist-
    ence of boards)
  Country Parks (c)
  Footpaths and Bridleways
  Commons—registration
  Caravan Sites—provision (c)
  Gipsy Sites—provision
  Smallholdings and Cottage Hold-
    ings

Highways and Related Subjects
  Transport Planning
  Highways
  Traffic
  Parking
  Public Transport (co-ordination)
  Road Safety
  Street Lighting

Non-Metropolitan Districts

Education and Related Services
  Museums and Art Galleries (c)

Housing and Town Development
  Housing
  Town Development

Town and Country Planning and
    Related Matters
  Local Plans (most)
  Development Control (most)
  Acquisition and Disposal of Land
  Clearance of Derelict Land (c)
  Country Parks (c)
  Footpaths and Bridleways
  Caravan Sites—provision (c) lic-
    ensing and management
  Gipsy Sites—management
  Allotments

Highways and Related Subjects
  Highways—can claim powers
    over unclassified roads in urban
    areas
  Public Transport—operation

Environmental Health
Food Safety and Hygiene
  Control of Communicable Disease
  Control of Office, Shop and Factory Premises

Consumer Protection
  Weights and Measures
  Food and Drugs
  Trade Descriptions
  Consumer Protection

Other Environmental Services
  Land Drainage
  Refuse Disposal
  Health Education (c)

Other Environmental Services
  Local Sewers
  Land Drainage
  Refuse Collection
  Litter
  Coast Protection
  Clean Air
  Building Regulations
  Street Cleansing
  Nuisances
  Cemeteries and Crematoria
  Markets
  Offensive Trades
  Health Education (c)

Police and Fire
  Police (subject to amalgamation)
  Fire

Recreation and Tourism
  Swimming Baths (c)
  Parks and Open Spaces (c)
  Physical Training and Recreation (c)

Recreation and Tourism
  Swimming Baths (c)
  Parks and Open Spaces (c)
  Physical Training and Recreation (c)
  Publicity for Tourist Attractions

Licensing and Registration Functions
  Births, Deaths and Marriages
  Adoption Societies

Licensing and Registration Functions

Other Services
  Entertainments (c)
  Aerodromes (c)
  Natural Emergencies (c)

Other Services
  Entertainments (c)
  Aerodromes (c)
  Natural Emergencies (c)

c = concurrent functions

This table ignores minor variations which may exist in Wales

178

Metropolitan Counties

Education and Related Services
  Museums and Art Galleries (c)

Housing and Town Development
  Certain reserve powers, e.g. over-
    spill
  Town Development

Town and Country Planning and
  Related Matters
  Structure Plans
  Local Plans (in special cases)
  Development Control (strategic
    and reserved decisions)
  Acquisition and Disposal of
    Land (c)
  Clearance of Derelict Land (c)
  National Parks (subject to exist-
    ence of boards)
  Country Parks (c)
  Footpaths and Bridleways
  Commons—registration
  Caravan Sites—provision (c)
  Gipsy Sites—provision
  Smallholdings and Cottage Hold-
    ings

Highways and Related Subjects
  Transport Planning
  Highways
  Traffic
  Parking
  Passenger Transport
  Road Safety

Consumer Protection
  Weights and Measures
  Food and Drugs
  Trade Descriptions
  Consumer Protection

Metropolitan Districts
Social Services

Education and Related Services
  Education
  Libraries
  Museums and Art Galleries (c)

Housing and Town Development
  Housing
  Town Development

Town and Country Planning and
  Related Matters
  Local Plans (most)
  Development Control (most)
  Acquisition and Disposal of
    Land (c)
  Clearance of Derelict Land (c)
  Country Parks (c)
  Footpaths and Bridleways
  Commons—management
  Caravan Sites—provision (c) lic-
    ensing and management
  Gipsy Sites—management

Highways and Related Subjects
  Highways—can claim mainten-
    ance powers over unclassified
    roads in urban areas

Environmental Health
  Food Safety and Hygiene
  Control of Communicable Dis-
    ease
  Control of Office, Shop and
    Factory Premises

Other Environmental Services
  Land Drainage
  Refuse Disposal
  Health Education (c)

Police and Fire
  Police (subject to amalgamation)
  Fire

Recreation and Tourism
  Swimming Baths (c)
  Parks and Open Spaces (c)
  Physical Training and Recreation
    (c)

Other Services
  Entertainments (c)
  Aerodromes (c)
  Natural Emergencies (c)

c = concurrent functions

Other Environmental Services
  Local Sewers
  Land Drainage
  Refuse Collection
  Litter
  Coast Protection
  Clean Air
  Building Regulations
  Nuisances
  Cemeteries and Crematoria
  Markets
  Offensive Trades
  Health Education (c)

Recreation and Tourism
  Swimming Baths (c)
  Parks and Open Spaces (c)
  Physical Training and Recreation
    (c)
  Publicity for Tourist Attractions

Licensing and Registration Functions

Other Services
  Entertainments (c)
  Aerodromes (c)
    Natural Emergencies (c)

FURTHER READING

THE HISTORICAL BACKGROUND

Dilys M. Hill, *Democratic Theory and Local Government* (Allen & Unwin, 1974).
Bryan Keith-Lucas and Peter G. Richards, *A History of Local Government in the Twentieth Century* (Allen & Unwin, 1978).
J. Redlich and F. W. Hirst, *The History of Local Government in England* edited by B. Keith-Lucas (Macmillan, 1958).
Bruce Wood, *The Process of Local Government Reform 1966–74* (Allen & Unwin, 1976).
Report of the Royal Commission (Chairman, Lord Redcliffe-Maud), Cmnd 4040, 3 Vols (HMSO, 1969).

THE BASIS OF THE SYSTEM

W. O. Hart and J. F. Garner, *Local Government and Administration* (Butterworths, 9th ed. 1973).
Peter G. Richards, *The Local Government Act 1972: Problems of Implementation* (Allen & Unwin, 1975).

COUNCILLORS AND POLICY MAKING

W. Grant, *Independent Local Politics in England and Wales* (Saxon House, 1977).
D. Green, *Power and Party in an English City* (Allen & Unwin, 1980).
Report of the Committee on the *Remuneration of Councillors*, Cmnd 7010 (HMSO 1977).

CENTRAL-LOCAL RELATIONS

J. A. G. Griffith, *Central Departments and Local Authorities* (Allen & Unwin, 1966).
Report by the Central Policy Review Staff on *Relations Between Central Government and Local Authorities* (HMSO, 1977).

PROBLEMS OF PARTICULAR FUNCTIONS

J. B. Cullingworth, *Town and Country Planning in Britain* (Allen & Unwin, 6th edition, 1976).
Maurice Kogan, *Educational Policy Making* (Allen & Unwin, 1975).
G. Marshall, *Policy and Government* (Methuen, 2nd edition, 1967).

FINANCE

N. P. Hepworth, *The Finance of Local Government* (Allen & Unwin, 4th edition, 1978).
A. H. Marshall, *Financial Management in Local Government* (Allen & Unwin, 1974).
Report of the Layfield Committee, *Local Government Finance,* Cmnd 6453 (HMSO, 1974).

MANAGEMENT AND STAFFING

R. J. Haynes, *Organisation Theory and Local Government* (Allen & Unwin, 1980).
K. P. Poole, *The Local Government Service in England and Wales* (Allen & Unwin, 1978).
Report of the Maud Committee, *The Management of Local Government* (HMSO, 1967).
Report of the Mallaby Committee, *The Staffing of Local Government* (HMSO, 1967).
Report of the Bains Committee, *The New Local Authorities: Management and Structure* (HMSO, 1972).

LOCAL GOVERNMENT AND SOCIETY

W. Hampton, *Democracy and Community* (OUP, 1970).
N. Lewis and B. Gateshill, *The Commission for Local Administration* (RIPA, 1978).
J. Stanyer, *Understanding Local Government* (Fontana, 1976).